Preface

The world of technology is ever-evolving, with new innovations and methodologies constantly reshaping the landscape. Among the critical skills in this dynamic field is the ability to conduct thorough system analysis and design. This discipline forms the backbone of successful software development, ensuring that systems are efficient, effective, and scalable. Whether you are a fresher stepping into the professional realm or an experienced individual looking to refine your expertise, mastering system analysis and design is indispensable.

This book, "System Analysis and Design Interview Guide," is meticulously crafted to serve as a comprehensive resource for those preparing to face interviews in this domain. The primary aim is to bridge the gap between theoretical knowledge and practical application, equipping you with the tools and confidence needed to excel in your interviews.

Why This Book?

Interviews can be daunting, especially in a field as nuanced as system analysis and design. The questions posed often test not only your knowledge but also your problem-solving abilities, critical thinking, and adaptability. This book addresses these challenges by providing:

1. **Structured Content:** Covers fundamental concepts, methodologies, tools, and real-world applications, ensuring a seamless learning experience.
2. **Comprehensive Coverage:** Includes detailed discussions on requirement analysis, system modelling, design patterns, UML diagrams, and more.
3. **Practical Insights:** Real-world scenarios and case studies enhance your ability to tackle interview questions framed around real-life problems.
4. **Interview Questions and Answers**: A compilation of common interview questions with detailed answers, categorized by difficulty level.

Who Should Use This Book?

This book is designed for a diverse audience, including:

- **Fresh Graduates**: If you are a recent graduate or a final-year student aspiring to enter the field of system analysis and design, this guide will help you build a strong foundation and prepare for your first job interview.
- **Experienced Professionals**: For those who are already working in the industry but wish to switch roles or advance their careers, this book offers advanced topics and complex scenarios to enhance your expertise.
- **Self-Learners**: Individuals who are passionate about learning and wish to gain knowledge independently will find this book an invaluable resource.

Final Thoughts

In the competitive world of technology, standing out requires more than just theoretical knowledge. It demands the ability to apply that knowledge effectively and demonstrate your problem-solving skills. "System Analysis and Design Interview Guide" is your trusted companion in this journey, offering the insights and preparation needed to succeed.

We wish you all the best in your career endeavours and hope this book helps you achieve your professional goals. Happy learning and successful interviewing!

Table of Contents

Chapter 1: Introduction to System Analysis and Design

1.1 Understanding Systems

1.1.1 Question: What is a system in the context of system analysis and design?
Answer: A system is a set of interrelated components working together to achieve a common goal by processing inputs into outputs in a systematic manner.

1.1.2 Question: What are the key components of a system?
Answer: The key components of a system include inputs, processes, outputs, feedback mechanisms, and the environment in which the system operates.

1.1.3 Question: Can you explain the difference between an open system and a closed system?
Answer: An open system interacts with its environment and adapts to changes, while a closed system is isolated from its environment and does not adapt to external changes.

1.1.4 Question: What is system analysis?
Answer: System analysis is the process of studying and understanding the existing system to identify its components and their relationships, and to define the requirements for a new or improved system.

1.1.5 Question: Why is system design important?
Answer: System design is crucial because it translates the requirements identified during system analysis into a blueprint for constructing the new system, ensuring it meets user needs and operates efficiently.

1.1.6 Question: What are the main objectives of system analysis?
Answer: The main objectives of system analysis are to understand the current system, identify problems and opportunities, gather requirements, and propose feasible solutions.

1.1.7 Question: What is the role of a systems analyst?
Answer: A systems analyst is responsible for researching, planning, coordinating, and recommending software and system choices to meet an organization's business requirements.

1.1.8 Question: What is feasibility study in system analysis?
Answer: A feasibility study evaluates the practicality and potential success of a proposed system, considering factors like technical, economic, legal, operational, and schedule feasibility.

1.1.9 Question: What are the types of feasibility studies?
Answer: The types include technical feasibility, economic feasibility, legal feasibility, operational feasibility, and schedule feasibility.

1.1.10 Question: What is the significance of requirement gathering?
Answer: Requirement gathering is essential as it captures the needs and expectations of users and stakeholders, ensuring that the system developed aligns with their requirements.

1.1.11 Question: What are functional requirements?
Answer: Functional requirements specify what the system should do, describing its functionality and features, such as tasks, data handling, and processing.

1.1.12 Question: What are non-functional requirements?
Answer: Non-functional requirements define the system's operational characteristics, including performance, usability, reliability, and security.

1.1.13 Question: What is a use case in system design?
Answer: A use case is a description of a system's behaviour as it responds to a request from a stakeholder or external system, illustrating functional requirements.

1.1.14 Question: What is a data flow diagram (DFD)?
Answer: A DFD is a graphical representation of data movement within a system, showing how data enters, is processed, and exits the system.

1.1.15 Question: What are the levels of DFD?
Answer: Levels of DFD include context diagrams (Level 0), which show the system boundaries, and detailed DFDs (Levels 1, 2, etc.), which break down processes further.

1.1.16 Question: What is system modelling?
Answer: System modelling involves creating abstract models of a system, using diagrams and other tools, to visualize and understand its structure and behaviour.

1.1.17 Question: What is object-oriented design (OOD)?
Answer: OOD is a method of design encompassing the concepts of objects and classes, promoting reuse and modularity by modelling systems based on real-world entities.

1.1.18 Question: What is a class diagram in UML?
Answer: A class diagram is a type of UML diagram that shows the static structure of a system, illustrating classes, their attributes, operations, and relationships.

1.1.19 Question: What is a sequence diagram in UML?
Answer: A sequence diagram is a UML diagram that shows how objects interact in a particular scenario of a use case, detailing the sequence of messages exchanged.

1.1.20 Question: What is the importance of design patterns?
Answer: Design patterns provide reusable solutions to common design problems, improving system maintainability, scalability, and reducing development time.

1.1.21 Question: What is a software architecture?
Answer: Software architecture is the high-level structure of a software system, defining its components, their relationships, and the principles guiding its design and evolution.

1.1.22 Question: What is the role of testing in system development?
Answer: Testing ensures that the system meets its requirements and functions correctly, identifying defects and verifying that the system performs as intended.

1.1.23 Question: What are the different types of testing?
Answer: Types of testing include unit testing, integration testing, system testing, acceptance testing, performance testing, and usability testing.

1.1.24 Question: What is system implementation?
Answer: System implementation is the process of deploying the designed system into the production environment, including coding, testing, installation, and training.

1.1.25 Question: What is system maintenance?
Answer: System maintenance involves making updates and improvements to the system after deployment, including fixing bugs, enhancing functionality, and adapting to changes.

1.1.26 Question: What is change management in system development?
Answer: Change management is the process of managing changes to a system in a controlled manner, ensuring they are implemented efficiently and with minimal disruption.

1.1.27 Question: What is the Agile methodology?
Answer: Agile is an iterative and incremental approach to software development that emphasizes flexibility, collaboration, and customer feedback.

1.1.28 Question: What is the Waterfall model?

Answer: The Waterfall model is a linear and sequential approach to software development, where each phase must be completed before the next begins.

1.1.29 Question: What is a Gantt chart?

Answer: A Gantt chart is a visual project management tool that illustrates the project schedule, showing tasks, durations, and dependencies.

1.1.30 Question: What is a critical path in project management?

Answer: The critical path is the longest sequence of tasks in a project plan, determining the shortest time to complete the project.

1.2 The System Development Lifecycle

1.2.1 Question: What is the System Development Lifecycle (SDLC)?

Answer: The SDLC is a structured approach used for developing information systems through various phases, including planning, analysis, design, implementation, and maintenance.

1.2.2 Question: What are the primary phases of the SDLC?

Answer: The primary phases are planning, analysis, design, implementation, testing, deployment, and maintenance.

1.2.3 Question: What is the purpose of the planning phase in SDLC?

Answer: The planning phase involves defining project goals, scope, constraints, resources, and timelines to ensure a clear and structured approach.

1.2.4 Question: What activities are conducted during the analysis phase?

Answer: During the analysis phase, requirements are gathered, documented, and analysed to understand what the system needs to accomplish.

1.2.5 Question: How does the design phase differ from the analysis phase?

Answer: The design phase translates the requirements identified in the analysis phase into detailed specifications for building the system, including architecture, components, and interfaces.

1.2.6 Question: What is system implementation?

Answer: System implementation involves coding, integrating, and deploying the system based on the design specifications.

1.2.7 Question: What is the role of testing in the SDLC?

Answer: Testing ensures the system functions correctly, meets requirements, and is free of defects through various levels such as unit, integration, system, and acceptance testing.

1.2.8 Question: What happens during the deployment phase?

Answer: The deployment phase involves installing the system in the production environment and making it available for use by end-users.

1.2.9 Question: Why is the maintenance phase important in SDLC?

Answer: The maintenance phase addresses any issues that arise post-deployment, including bug fixes, updates, and enhancements to ensure the system continues to meet user needs.

1.2.10 Question: What is the Waterfall model?

Answer: The Waterfall model is a linear and sequential SDLC approach where each phase must be completed before moving on to the next, with no overlap.

1.2.11 Question: How does the Agile methodology differ from the Waterfall model?

Answer: Agile is an iterative and incremental approach that promotes flexibility, customer collaboration, and continuous delivery, unlike the rigid, sequential Waterfall model.

1.2.12 Question: What is a feasibility study in the SDLC?
Answer: A feasibility study evaluates the practicality and potential success of a proposed project, considering technical, economic, legal, operational, and schedule aspects.

1.2.13 Question: What is the role of a project manager in the SDLC?
Answer: A project manager oversees the project, ensuring it stays on track, within scope, budget, and meets the defined objectives and timelines.

1.2.14 Question: What is a prototype in system development?
Answer: A prototype is an early, simplified version of a system used to visualize and test design ideas, gather feedback, and refine requirements.

1.2.15 Question: What is the V-Model in SDLC?
Answer: The V-Model is an extension of the Waterfall model that emphasizes verification and validation, with corresponding testing activities for each development phase.

1.2.16 Question: What is the Spiral model?
Answer: The Spiral model combines iterative development with systematic aspects of the Waterfall model, focusing on risk assessment and iterative refinement through repeated cycles.

1.2.17 Question: How is risk management integrated into the SDLC?
Answer: Risk management involves identifying, analysing, and mitigating risks throughout the SDLC to minimize potential issues and ensure project success.

1.2.18 Question: What is a use case in system design?
Answer: A use case describes how users interact with a system to achieve a specific goal, detailing the functional requirements from the user's perspective.

1.2.19 Question: What is the significance of requirement documentation?
Answer: Requirement documentation captures user needs and expectations clearly, serving as a reference throughout the SDLC to ensure the system meets its intended purpose.

1.2.20 Question: What are non-functional requirements?
Answer: Non-functional requirements define system attributes such as performance, security, usability, and reliability, influencing the overall user experience.

1.2.21 Question: What is change management in system development?
Answer: Change management controls and manages changes to the system during development, ensuring they are implemented smoothly without disrupting project progress.

1.2.22 Question: What is the role of user training in system deployment?
Answer: User training ensures that end-users understand how to use the system effectively, facilitating a smooth transition and maximizing the system's benefits.

1.2.23 Question: What is version control in software development?
Answer: Version control tracks and manages changes to software code, enabling collaboration among developers and maintaining the integrity of the project.

1.2.24 Question: What is a Gantt chart used for in project management?
Answer: A Gantt chart visually represents the project schedule, showing tasks, durations, and dependencies to aid in planning and tracking progress.

1.2.25 Question: How does integration testing differ from unit testing?

Answer: Integration testing verifies the interactions between system components, while unit testing focuses on individual components or units of the system.

1.2.26 Question: What is user acceptance testing (UAT)?
Answer: UAT involves end-users testing the system in a real-world environment to ensure it meets their needs and performs as expected before final deployment.

1.2.27 Question: What is the importance of scalability in system design?
Answer: Scalability ensures that the system can handle increased load or demand without compromising performance, supporting future growth and changes.

1.2.28 Question: What is a context diagram?
Answer: A context diagram is a high-level DFD showing the system boundaries, external entities interacting with the system, and data flows between them.

1.2.29 Question: What is an entity-relationship diagram (ERD)?
Answer: An ERD is a graphical representation of entities and their relationships in a database, used for data modelling.

1.2.30 Question: What is system integration?
Answer: System integration involves combining different subsystems or components into a single, unified system, ensuring they work together seamlessly.

1.2.31 Question: What is the purpose of system documentation?
Answer: System documentation provides detailed information about the system's design, functionality, and usage, supporting development, maintenance, and user training.

1.2.32 Question: What is a sequence diagram in UML?
Answer: A sequence diagram is a UML diagram that shows how objects interact in a particular scenario of a use case, detailing the sequence of messages exchanged.

1.2.33 Question: What is a flowchart?
Answer: A flowchart is a diagram that represents the flow of a process or system using symbols and arrows, illustrating steps and decision points.

1.2.34 Question: What is the importance of system architecture?
Answer: System architecture defines the high-level structure of a system, outlining components, their relationships, and guiding principles for its design and evolution.

1.2.35 Question: What is the role of feedback in the SDLC?
Answer: Feedback helps identify issues, improve system functionality, and ensure continuous improvement throughout the SDLC.

1.2.36 Question: What are design patterns in software development?
Answer: Design patterns are reusable solutions to common design problems, improving system maintainability and reducing development time.

1.3 Roles and Responsibilities in System Development

1.3.1 Question: What is the role of a systems analyst?
Answer: A systems analyst is responsible for researching, planning, coordinating, and recommending software and system choices to meet an organization's business requirements.

1.3.2 Question: What are the primary responsibilities of a systems analyst?
Answer: Responsibilities include gathering and analysinguser requirements, creating system specifications, designing system models, and coordinating with development teams.

1.3.3 Question: How does a systems analyst contribute to project success?
Answer: By ensuring clear communication between stakeholders and the development team, a systems analyst helps ensure that the final system meets user needs and business goals.

1.3.4 Question: What is the role of a project manager in system development?
Answer: A project manager oversees the planning, execution, and completion of a project, ensuring it meets deadlines, stays within budget, and achieves its objectives.

1.3.5 Question: What are the key responsibilities of a project manager?
Answer: Key responsibilities include project planning, resource allocation, risk management, and coordinating tasks across the project team.

1.3.6 Question: What is the role of a software developer in system development?
Answer: A software developer is responsible for writing code, developing applications, and implementing system designs according to the specifications provided by the systems analyst.

1.3.7 Question: What are the primary tasks of a software developer?
Answer: Primary tasks include coding, debugging, testing, and documenting software applications, as well as collaborating with other developers and stakeholders.

1.3.8 Question: What is the role of a quality assurance (QA) analyst in system development?
Answer: A QA analyst ensures that the software meets quality standards by planning and executing tests, identifying defects, and verifying fixes.

1.3.9 Question: What are the key responsibilities of a QA analyst?
Answer: Key responsibilities include creating test plans, writing test cases, executing tests, and reporting defects to the development team.

1.3.10 Question: What is the role of a database administrator (DBA)?
Answer: A DBA is responsible for managing and maintaining an organization's databases, ensuring data integrity, performance, and security.

1.3.11 Question: What are the primary responsibilities of a database administrator?
Answer: Responsibilities include database design, implementation, backup and recovery, performance tuning, and ensuring data security.

1.3.12 Question: What is the role of a business analyst in system development?
Answer: A business analyst identifies business needs and translates them into technical requirements, bridging the gap between stakeholders and the development team.

1.3.13 Question: What are the key tasks of a business analyst?
Answer: Key tasks include conducting stakeholder interviews, analysingbusiness processes, defining requirements, and creating functional specifications.

1.3.14 Question: What is the role of a user experience (UX) designer in system development?
Answer: A UX designer focuses on creating user-friendly interfaces that enhance user satisfaction and usability.

1.3.15 Question: What are the primary responsibilities of a UX designer?
Answer: Responsibilities include conducting user research, creating wireframes and prototypes, and collaborating with developers to implement design solutions.

1.3.16 Question: What is the role of a system architect?
Answer: A system architect designs the overall structure of the system, ensuring it meets technical and business requirements.

1.3.17 Question: What are the key responsibilities of a system architect?
Answer: Responsibilities include creating architectural blueprints, selecting technology stacks, and ensuring scalability and maintainability of the system.

1.3.18 Question: What is the role of a network administrator in system development?
Answer: A network administrator manages an organization's network infrastructure, ensuring reliable and secure connectivity.

1.3.19 Question: What are the primary tasks of a network administrator?
Answer: Primary tasks include configuring network hardware, monitoring network performance, and troubleshooting connectivity issues.

1.3.20 Question: What is the role of a security analyst in system development?
Answer: A security analyst protects the system from cyber threats by implementing security measures and monitoring for potential breaches.

1.3.21 Question: What are the key responsibilities of a security analyst?
Answer: Responsibilities include conducting security assessments, developing security policies, and responding to security incidents.

1.3.22 Question: What is the role of a change manager in system development?
Answer: A change manager oversees the process of managing changes to the system, ensuring they are implemented smoothly and with minimal disruption.

1.3.23 Question: What are the primary tasks of a change manager?
Answer: Primary tasks include evaluating change requests, coordinating change implementation, and communicating changes to stakeholders.

1.3.24 Question: What is the role of a product owner in Agile development?
Answer: A product owner defines the product vision, prioritizes features, and ensures the development team delivers value to the business.

1.3.25 Question: What are the key responsibilities of a product owner?
Answer: Responsibilities include creating and managing the product backlog, defining user stories, and collaborating with the development team.

1.3.26 Question: What is the role of a Scrum Master in Agile development?
Answer: A Scrum Master facilitates Agile practices, ensures the team follows Scrum processes, and removes impediments to progress.

1.3.27 Question: What are the primary tasks of a Scrum Master?
Answer: Primary tasks include organizing Scrum meetings, coaching the team on Agile practices, and addressing obstacles.

1.3.28 Question: What is the role of an IT support specialist?
Answer: An IT support specialist provides technical assistance to users, troubleshooting hardware and software issues.

1.3.29 Question: What are the key responsibilities of an IT support specialist?
Answer: Responsibilities include resolving user problems, maintaining IT systems, and providing training on new technologies.

1.3.30 Question: What is the role of a technical writer in system development?
Answer: A technical writer creates documentation that explains how to use and maintain the system, ensuring clear and concise communication.

1.3.31 Question: What are the primary tasks of a technical writer?
Answer: Primary tasks include writing user manuals, creating help guides, and producing technical specifications.

1.3.32 Question: What is the role of a DevOps engineer?
Answer: A DevOps engineer bridges development and operations, automating and streamlining processes to improve system reliability and performance.

1.3.33 Question: What are the key responsibilities of a DevOps engineer?
Answer: Responsibilities include automating deployments, monitoring system performance, and collaborating with development and operations teams.

1.3.34 Question: What is the role of a configuration manager in system development?
Answer: A configuration manager ensures that system configurations are maintained consistently and accurately throughout the development lifecycle.

1.3.35 Question: What are the primary tasks of a configuration manager?
Answer: Primary tasks include managing configuration items, maintaining version control, and documenting configuration changes.

1.3.36 Question: What is the role of a performance analyst in system development?
Answer: A performance analyst evaluates system performance, identifying bottlenecks and recommending improvements.

1.3.37 Question: What are the key responsibilities of a performance analyst?
Answer: Responsibilities include conducting performance tests, analysingresults, and optimizing system performance.

1.3.38 Question: What is the role of a data analyst in system development?
Answer: A data analyst interprets data to provide insights and support decision-making processes within the system development project.

1.3.39 Question: What are the primary tasks of a data analyst?
Answer: Primary tasks include data collection, analysis, reporting, and visualizing data to inform stakeholders.

1.3.40 Question: What is the role of an end-user in system development?
Answer: End-users are the individuals who use the final system, providing feedback and identifying areas for improvement.

1.4 Trends and Challenges in System Analysis and Design

1.4.1 Question: What are some current trends in system analysis and design?
Answer: Current trends include the adoption of Agile and DevOps methodologies, increased use of automation tools, emphasis on user experience design, and the integration of artificial intelligence and machine learning.

1.4.2 Question: How is Agile methodology influencing system analysis and design?
Answer: Agile promotes iterative development, collaboration, and flexibility, allowing for rapid adaptation to changing requirements and continuous delivery of valuable software.

1.4.3 Question: What is the impact of DevOps on system development?
Answer: DevOps bridges the gap between development and operations, fostering a culture of collaboration and continuous integration/delivery, leading to faster and more reliable software releases.

1.4.4 Question: How are automation tools changing system analysis and design?

Answer: Automation tools streamline tasks such as testing, deployment, and monitoring, reducing manual effort, improving accuracy, and accelerating the development process.

1.4.5 Question: What is the role of user experience (UX) in system design?
Answer: UX focuses on creating systems that are intuitive, accessible, and satisfying to use, enhancing user satisfaction and overall system effectiveness.

1.4.6 Question: How is AI being integrated into system analysis and design?
Answer: AI is used to automate analysis, optimize design processes, predict system behaviour, and enhance decision-making through advanced data analytics and machine learning algorithms.

1.4.7 Question: What are some challenges in adopting new technologies in system design?
Answer: Challenges include managing the complexity of integration, ensuring data security, maintaining scalability, and addressing skill gaps in the workforce.

1.4.8 Question: How does cloud computing affect system design?
Answer: Cloud computing offers scalable resources, reduces infrastructure costs, and supports flexible, distributed system architectures, but requires careful planning for security and compliance.

1.4.9 Question: What is the importance of cybersecurity in system analysis and design?
Answer: Ensuring robust cybersecurity measures is critical to protect systems from breaches, data loss, and other security threats, safeguarding sensitive information and maintaining user trust.

1.4.10 Question: How do microservices architecture impact system design?
Answer: Microservices architecture allows for building scalable, modular systems where each service can be developed, deployed, and scaled independently, improving flexibility and resilience.

1.4.11 Question: What are the benefits of using big data in system analysis?
Answer: Big data enables the analysis of vast amounts of data for insights, improving decision-making, enhancing system performance, and enabling predictive analytics.

1.4.12 Question: How do regulatory requirements influence system design?
Answer: Regulatory requirements ensure compliance with laws and standards, affecting system design through data protection, security measures, and ensuring ethical usage of information.

1.4.13 Question: What are the challenges of maintaining legacy systems?
Answer: Challenges include integrating with modern technologies, high maintenance costs, limited flexibility, and the scarcity of expertise in outdated technologies.

1.4.14 Question: How is the Internet of Things (IoT) influencing system design?
Answer: IoT requires designing systems that can handle large-scale data from connected devices, ensure real-time processing, and maintain robust security and privacy measures.

1.4.15 Question: What is the impact of digital transformation on system analysis and design?
Answer: Digital transformation drives the need for innovative system designs that leverage new technologies, improve user experiences, and support business agility and competitiveness.

1.4.16 Question: How do data privacy concerns affect system design?
Answer: Data privacy concerns necessitate incorporating robust data protection measures, ensuring compliance with privacy regulations, and designing systems that respect user data rights.

1.4.17 Question: What are the challenges of designing for mobile platforms?
Answer: Challenges include ensuring responsive design, optimizing performance, managing diverse device specifications, and maintaining security across different mobile operating systems.

1.4.18 Question: How does globalization impact system design?

Answer: Globalization requires designing systems that support multiple languages, cultural contexts, legal requirements, and time zones, ensuring accessibility and usability worldwide.

1.4.19 Question: What is the significance of sustainable system design?
Answer: Sustainable system design focuses on reducing environmental impact through energy-efficient systems, sustainable resource usage, and promoting long-term ecological balance.

1.4.20 Question: How does the rise of remote work influence system design?
Answer: Remote work necessitates designing systems that support remote access, collaboration, secure data sharing, and maintaining productivity and communication across distributed teams.

1.4.21 Question: What are the challenges of real-time data processing?
Answer: Challenges include ensuring low-latency processing, managing high data volumes, maintaining data accuracy, and ensuring system scalability and reliability.

1.4.22 Question: How do AI ethics impact system design?
Answer: AI ethics require designing systems that ensure fairness, transparency, accountability, and avoid biases, promoting ethical use of AI technologies.

1.4.23 Question: What is the role of blockchain in system design?
Answer: Blockchain provides decentralized, secure, and transparent systems, enhancing data integrity and trust, particularly in transactions and record-keeping applications.

1.4.24 Question: How does edge computing affect system design?
Answer: Edge computing involves processing data closer to the source, reducing latency, improving response times, and enabling real-time applications, particularly in IoT systems.

1.4.25 Question: What are the challenges of integrating third-party APIs?
Answer: Challenges include ensuring compatibility, managing security risks, handling version updates, and ensuring reliable performance and data integrity.

1.4.26 Question: How does machine learning impact system analysis?
Answer: Machine learning enhances system analysis by providing predictive insights, automating data analysis, identifying patterns, and improving decision-making processes.

1.4.27 Question: What is the importance of scalability in modern systems?
Answer: Scalability ensures that a system can handle increasing loads or growth in users without compromising performance, supporting business expansion and future demands.

1.4.28 Question: How do user feedback mechanisms improve system design?
Answer: User feedback mechanisms gather insights from real users, informing iterative improvements, enhancing user satisfaction, and ensuring the system meets user needs.

1.4.29 Question: What are the trends in data visualization for system analysis?
Answer: Trends include interactive dashboards, real-time data visualization, use of AI for automated insights, and advanced tools for complex data representation, aiding better decision-making.

1.4.30 Question: How does continuous integration/continuous delivery (CI/CD) influence system development?
Answer: CI/CD practices streamline the development process, enabling frequent and reliable releases, reducing errors, and improving overall system quality and responsiveness.

1.4.31 Question: What are the challenges of designing multi-cloud systems?
Answer: Challenges include ensuring interoperability, managing security across different providers, optimizing costs, and maintaining performance and reliability.

1.4.32 Question: How does user-centric design benefit system development?

Answer: User-centric design focuses on the needs and experiences of the end-users, leading to more intuitive, accessible, and effective systems that meet user expectations.

1.4.33 Question: What is the role of DevSecOps in system development?
Answer: DevSecOps integrates security practices into the DevOps pipeline, ensuring that security is considered at every stage of development, leading to more secure systems.

1.4.34 Question: How does API-first design impact system integration?
Answer: API-first design prioritizes the development of robust and scalable APIs, facilitating seamless integration, modularity, and interoperability between different systems.

1.4.35 Question: What is the significance of data governance in system design?
Answer: Data governance ensures that data is managed properly, maintaining quality, consistency, and compliance with regulations, supporting reliable and secure system operations.

Online Resources

More Practices Questions

Online Exam Paper
URL
https://forms.gle/2PUDZ1zYzMDRn9hD7

QR Code

YouTube Video Playlist Link

Chapter 1
URL
https://www.youtube.com/playlist?list=PLzlh_31VWEFqeTtpvodYxhOEnUFr0Nzq-

QR Code

Chapter 2: Systems Thinking and Concepts

2.1 Solving Principles of Systems Thinking

2.1.1 Question: What are systems thinking?
Answer: Systems thinking is an approach to problem-solving that views problems as part of an overall system, rather than in isolation, emphasizing the interconnections and interactions within the system.

2.1.2 Question: How does systems thinking differ from traditional analysis?
Answer: Traditional analysis breaks down systems into individual parts, while systems thinking focuses on the interactions and relationships between parts to understand the system as a whole.

2.1.3 Question: What are the key principles of systems thinking?
Answer: Key principles include interconnectivity, feedback loops, adaptation, and understanding the system's environment and boundaries.

2.1.4 Question: What is a feedback loop in systems thinking?
Answer: A feedback loop is a cycle where outputs of a system are fed back as inputs, influencing future outputs. They can be reinforcing (positive) or balancing (negative).

2.1.5 Question: Can you explain the concept of interconnectivity in systems thinking?
Answer: Interconnectivity refers to how different components of a system are linked and influence each other, emphasizing the importance of understanding these connections to address system-wide issues.

2.1.6 Question: What is the importance of boundaries in systems thinking?
Answer: Boundaries define the limits of a system, determining what is included or excluded, and help in focusing analysis on relevant interactions and components.

2.1.7 Question: What is a system archetype?
Answer: A system archetype is a common pattern of behaviour in systems that can help identify recurring issues and guide interventions to address them.

2.1.8 Question: Give an example of a common system archetype.
Answer: An example is "Limits to Growth," where initial success leads to growth that eventually hits a limit due to constraints, causing performance to plateau or decline.

2.1.9 Question: What is the role of leverage points in systems thinking?
Answer: Leverage points are strategic places within a system where a small change can lead to significant improvements, helping to effectively address complex problems.

2.1.10 Question: How can systems thinking improve decision-making?
Answer: Systems thinking improves decision-making by providing a holistic view, considering long-term impacts and interactions, and identifying root causes of problems.

2.1.11 Question: What is the significance of mental models in systems thinking?
Answer: Mental models are internal representations of reality that influence how individuals understand and interact with systems. Updating these models can lead to better problem-solving and decision-making.

2.1.12 Question: What is dynamic complexity?
Answer: Dynamic complexity refers to situations where cause and effect are not immediately obvious due to delays, feedback loops, and non-linear relationships within the system.

2.1.13 Question: How does systems thinking help in managing dynamic complexity?
Answer: Systems thinking helps manage dynamic complexity by emphasizing the understanding of feedback loops, delays, and interactions, enabling more effective interventions.

2.1.14 Question: What is the iceberg model in systems thinking?
Answer: The iceberg model is a tool that illustrates how underlying structures and mental models (below the surface) drive visible events and patterns (above the surface).

2.1.15 Question: Why is understanding the system's environment important?
Answer: Understanding the system's environment is crucial as it affects the system's behaviour and performance, helping in identifying external factors that influence the system.

2.1.16 Question: What is a causal loop diagram (CLD)?
Answer: A CLD is a visual representation of the feedback loops within a system, showing the relationships between variables and how they influence each other.

2.1.17 Question: How do balancing loops function in a system?
Answer: Balancing loops counteract changes in a system, promoting stability by bringing the system back to equilibrium when it deviates from a desired state.

2.1.18 Question: What is the purpose of system dynamics modelling?
Answer: System dynamics modelling aims to understand and simulate the behaviour of complex systems over time, using feedback loops and time delays to analyse how systems change.

2.1.19 Question: What is meant by 'holistic view' in systems thinking?
Answer: A holistic view involves looking at the entire system and its interactions rather than focusing on individual components, providing a comprehensive understanding of how the system functions.

2.1.20 Question: How does systems thinking facilitate problem-solving?
Answer: Systems thinking facilitates problem-solving by identifying root causes, understanding the interdependencies, and considering the long-term effects of solutions.

2.1.21 Question: What is the significance of resilience in a system?
Answer: Resilience is the ability of a system to adapt and recover from disruptions, ensuring its sustainability and long-term functionality.

2.1.22 Question: How do reinforcing loops affect a system?
Answer: Reinforcing loops amplify changes in a system, leading to exponential growth or decline, depending on the nature of the feedback.

2.1.23 Question: What is the difference between a system map and a causal loop diagram?
Answer: A system map shows the components and their connections in a system, while a causal loop diagram focuses on the feedback loops and relationships between variables.

2.1.24 Question: How does systems thinking contribute to sustainable development?
Answer: Systems thinking contributes to sustainable development by promoting a long-term perspective, understanding ecological and social interactions, and identifying leverage points for sustainable solutions.

2.1.25 Question: What is the role of scenarios in systems thinking?
Answer: Scenarios help explore different future possibilities, allowing stakeholders to understand potential outcomes and prepare for various contingencies.

2.1.26 Question: What is a stock and flow diagram?
Answer: A stock and flow diagram is a visual tool used in system dynamics to represent stocks (accumulations) and flows (rates of change) within a system.

2.1.27 Question: How does systems thinking enhance organizational learning?
Answer: Systems thinking enhances organizational learning by encouraging a deeper understanding of interdependencies, fostering collaboration, and promoting continuous improvement.

2.1.28 Question: What is the principle of leverage in systems thinking?
Answer: The principle of leverage involves identifying points within a system where a small change can lead to significant improvements, making interventions more effective.

2.1.29 Question: How can systems thinking be applied in project management?
Answer: Systems thinking can be applied in project management by understanding the interdependencies between project elements, managing risks, and ensuring alignment with organizational goals.

2.1.30 Question: What is the role of feedback in systems thinking?
Answer: Feedback in systems thinking provides information on the outcomes of actions, allowing for adjustments and improvements in system performance.

2.1.31 Question: How does systems thinking approach complex problems?
Answer: Systems thinking approaches complex problems by considering the entire system, identifying root causes, and addressing interactions and feedback loops.

2.1.32 Question: What is the impact of time delays in systems?
Answer: Time delays can cause discrepancies between actions and outcomes, leading to unintended consequences and complicating system behaviour analysis.

2.1.33 Question: Why are mental models important in systems thinking?
Answer: Mental models shape how individuals perceive and respond to systems, influencing decision-making and problem-solving effectiveness.

2.1.34 Question: What is the concept of 'emergence' in systems thinking?
Answer: Emergence refers to the behaviour of a system that arises from the interactions of its components, often producing unexpected outcomes.

2.1.35 Question: How can systems thinking improve healthcare systems?
Answer: Systems thinking can improve healthcare systems by understanding patient flows, identifying bottlenecks, and designing interventions that enhance overall system efficiency.

2.1.36 Question: What is the value of visual tools in systems thinking?
Answer: Visual tools, such as diagrams and maps, help illustrate complex relationships, making it easier to understand and communicate system behaviour.

2.1.37 Question: How does systems thinking relate to strategic planning?
Answer: Systems thinking relates to strategic planning by providing a holistic view, identifying leverage points, and considering long-term impacts to achieve sustainable success.

2.1.38 Question: What is the significance of adaptation in systems?
Answer: Adaptation allows systems to adjust to changes in their environment, ensuring their continued effectiveness and resilience.

2.1.39 Question: How do non-linear relationships affect systems?
Answer: Non-linear relationships can cause disproportionate effects, where small changes lead to significant outcomes, complicating prediction and control of system behaviour.

2.1.40 Question: What is the importance of continuous feedback in systems thinking?
Answer: Continuous feedback provides ongoing information on system performance, enabling timely adjustments and improvements for better outcomes.

2.2 Systems Theory and Concepts

2.2.1 Question: What is the importance of interconnectivity in systems?

Answer: Interconnectivity ensures that different components of a system can communicate and work together, enhancing overall functionality and adaptability.

2.2.2 Question: Can you explain systems theory?
Answer: Systems theory is an interdisciplinary study of systems, exploring their structures, behaviours, and interactions, aiming to understand complex interrelationships.

2.2.3 Question: What is a subsystem?
Answer: A subsystem is a smaller component of a larger system, functioning independently but contributing to the overall objectives of the parent system.

2.2.4 Question: What is a system boundary?
Answer: A system boundary defines the limits of a system, distinguishing between the system itself and its environment or external systems.

2.2.5 Question: What is feedback in a system?
Answer: Feedback is the process by which a system self-regulates by using its output as input to adjust and control its behaviour and performance.

2.2.6 Question: What are open systems?
Answer: Open systems are systems that interact with their environment, exchanging energy, materials, and information, and adapting to changes.

2.2.7 Question: What are closed systems?
Answer: Closed systems do not interact with their environment and are isolated from external influences, relying only on internal mechanisms.

2.2.8 Question: What is system dynamics?
Answer: System dynamics is a methodology for understanding the behaviour of complex systems over time, using feedback loops and time delays.

2.2.9 Question: What is the principle of equifinality?
Answer: The principle of equifinality suggests that a system can reach the same final state from different initial conditions and through various paths.

2.2.10 Question: What is an emergent property?
Answer: An emergent property is a characteristic of a system that arises from the interaction of its components, which cannot be deduced from the properties of individual components.

2.2.11 Question: What is holism in systems theory?
Answer: Holism is the concept that a system should be viewed as a whole, rather than merely as a collection of its parts, emphasizing interdependencies.

2.2.12 Question: What is a feedback loop?
Answer: A feedback loop is a system structure that causes output from one node to eventually influence input to that same node, either positively (reinforcing) or negatively (balancing).

2.2.13 Question: What is system modelling in systems theory?
Answer: System modelling involves creating abstract representations of a system to study its components and interactions, aiding in understanding and predicting behaviour.

2.2.14 Question: What is a causal loop diagram?
Answer: A causal loop diagram is a tool used in system dynamics to visualize how variables in a system are interrelated through feedback loops.

2.2.15 Question: What is homeostasis in a system?

Answer: Homeostasis is the ability of a system to maintain stability and equilibrium by adjusting its internal processes in response to external changes.

2.2.16 Question: What is system resilience?
Answer: System resilience is the capacity of a system to absorb disturbances and still retain its basic structure and functions.

2.2.17 Question: What is a complex adaptive system?
Answer: A complex adaptive system is a system composed of interconnected, adaptive agents whose interactions lead to emergent behaviours and self-organization.

2.2.18 Question: What is system optimization?
Answer: System optimization involves adjusting the elements of a system to achieve the best possible performance according to defined criteria.

2.2.19 Question: What is the difference between a system and an environment?
Answer: A system is a set of interacting components working towards a common goal, while the environment encompasses external factors and influences that affect the system.

2.2.20 Question: What is system decomposition?
Answer: System decomposition is the process of breaking down a complex system into smaller, more manageable subsystems or components.

2.2.21 Question: What is system integration?
Answer: System integration is the process of combining different subsystems or components into a single, cohesive system, ensuring they work together seamlessly.

2.2.22 Question: What is a system archetype?
Answer: A system archetype is a common pattern of behaviour found in systems, used to understand and anticipate recurring problems and dynamics.

2.2.23 Question: What is the law of requisite variety?
Answer: The law of requisite variety states that the complexity of a system's control mechanism must be equal to or greater than the complexity of the environment it operates in.

2.2.24 Question: What is the difference between hard and soft systems thinking?
Answer: Hard systems thinking focuses on technical, structured problems with clear solutions, while soft systems thinking deals with unstructured, human-centric issues requiring flexible approaches.

2.2.25 Question: What is an information system?
Answer: An information system is a set of components for collecting, storing, and processing data, providing information, and supporting decision-making.

2.2.26 Question: What is systems engineering?
Answer: Systems engineering is an interdisciplinary approach to designing, integrating, and managing complex systems throughout their life cycles.

2.2.27 Question: What is systems analysis?
Answer: Systems analysis involves studying a system to understand its components, functions, and interactions, often to identify problems and propose solutions.

2.2.28 Question: What is a system life cycle?
Answer: The system life cycle is the series of phases a system goes through from conception and development to operation and decommissioning.

2.2.29 Question: What is systemic risk?

Answer: Systemic risk is the potential for a system-wide failure due to the interconnectedness and interdependencies within a system.

2.2.30 Question: What is system sustainability?
Answer: System sustainability is the ability of a system to maintain its functions and processes over the long term without depleting resources or causing harm.

2.2.31 Question: What is a socio-technical system?
Answer: A socio-technical system is an approach that considers both social and technical aspects when designing and implementing systems, recognizing their interdependence.

2.2.32 Question: What is system robustness?
Answer: System robustness refers to the strength and resilience of a system to withstand and perform under various conditions without failing.

2.2.33 Question: What is a boundary object?
Answer: A boundary object is an artifact used in different ways by different communities but understood across these groups, facilitating collaboration and communication.

2.2.34 Question: What is systems mapping?
Answer: Systems mapping is the process of visually representing the components, relationships, and dynamics of a system to better understand and communicate its structure and behaviour.

2.2.35 Question: What is a leverage point in a system?
Answer: A leverage point is a strategic place within a system where a small shift can lead to significant changes in behaviour or outcomes.

2.2.36 Question: What is system validation?
Answer: System validation is the process of ensuring that a system meets the needs and requirements of its stakeholders, often involving testing and review.

2.2.37 Question: What is system verification?
Answer: System verification involves checking that a system conforms to its specifications and design, ensuring it was built correctly.

2.2.38 Question: What is systems theory's impact on organizational change?
Answer: Systems theory provides a framework for understanding the complex interrelationships within an organization, guiding effective change management by addressing systemic issues.

2.2.39 Question: What is a feedback control system?
Answer: A feedback control system uses feedback to maintain a desired state by comparing actual performance with a standard and making necessary adjustments.

2.3 Applying Systems Thinking to Problem

2.3.1 Question: How can systems thinking enhance organizational learning?
Answer: Systems thinking promotes a deeper understanding of organizational dynamics, encouraging continuous improvement and adaptive learning.

2.3.2 Question: How does systems thinking differ from traditional problem-solving?
Answer: Systems thinking focuses on understanding the interrelationships and dynamics within the entire system, while traditional problem-solving often targets isolated issues.

2.3.3 Question: What are the key principles of systems thinking?
Answer: Key principles include interconnectedness, feedback loops, holistic view, and causality within systems.

2.3.4 Question: Can you explain the concept of feedback loops in systems thinking?
Answer: Feedback loops are circular chains of cause and effect that influence the behaviour of the system. They can be reinforcing (amplifying) or balancing (stabilizing).

2.3.5 Question: What is a reinforcing feedback loop?
Answer: A reinforcing feedback loop amplifies changes, leading to exponential growth or decline within the system.

2.3.6 Question: What is a balancing feedback loop?
Answer: A balancing feedback loop counteracts changes, promoting stability and equilibrium within the system.

2.3.7 Question: Why is it important to identify feedback loops in a system?
Answer: Identifying feedback loops helps in understanding system dynamics and predicting how changes will affect the overall system behaviour.

2.3.8 Question: What is leverage in systems thinking?
Answer: Leverage is the point in a system where a small change can lead to significant impacts on the overall system.

2.3.9 Question: How can leverage points be used in problem-solving?
Answer: By identifying and acting on leverage points, you can achieve more effective and efficient solutions with minimal effort.

2.3.10 Question: What is the importance of a holistic view in systems thinking?
Answer: A holistic view considers the entire system and its interactions, ensuring that solutions address root causes rather than symptoms.

2.3.11 Question: Can you give an example of applying systems thinking in software development?
Answer: In software development, systems thinking can help identify how different modules interact and influence each other, leading to better integration and fewer bugs.

2.3.12 Question: What is the significance of boundary setting in systems thinking?
Answer: Boundary setting defines the scope of the system, ensuring a focused analysis and avoiding the inclusion of irrelevant elements.

2.3.13 Question: What is the "limits to growth" archetype?
Answer: The "limits to growth" archetype describes a situation were growth faces constraints, leading to a plateau or decline.

2.3.14 Question: How does the "shifting the burden" archetype affect problem-solving?
Answer: "Shifting the burden" occurs when short-term solutions are used to address symptoms, diverting attention from long-term solutions that tackle root causes.

2.3.15 Question: What is the "tragedy of the commons"?
Answer: The "tragedy of the commons" describes a situation where individuals acting in their own interest deplete shared resources, harming the whole group.

2.3.16 Question: How can systems thinking prevent the "tragedy of the commons"?
Answer: Systems thinking can identify collective impacts and promote sustainable practices, balancing individual needs with the well-being of the community.

2.3.17 Question: What is a causal loop diagram?
Answer: A causal loop diagram is a visual representation of the feedback loops within a system, showing the relationships between system variables.

2.3.18 Question: How do causal loop diagrams aid in problem-solving?
Answer: Causal loop diagrams help visualize system dynamics, identify feedback loops, and understand the complex interactions affecting the system.

2.3.19 Question: What is the purpose of system mapping?
Answer: System mapping is used to visually represent the components and interactions within a system, aiding in analysis and decision-making.

2.3.20 Question: What is mental model in systems thinking?
Answer: A mental model is an individual's internal representation of how a system works, influencing their understanding and decision-making.

2.3.21 Question: How can mental models be used to improve system performance?
Answer: By aligning mental models with actual system behaviour, individuals can make more informed and effective decisions.

2.3.22 Question: What is the significance of delays in systems thinking?
Answer: Delays in a system can affect the timing and effectiveness of interventions, making it crucial to anticipate and manage them.

2.3.23 Question: How can systems thinking help manage project risks?
Answer: Systems thinking can identify potential risks and their interconnections, enabling proactive management and mitigation strategies.

2.3.24 Question: What is the "fixes that fail" archetype?
Answer: The "fixes that fail" archetype describes a situation where quick fixes solve immediate problems but create long-term issues.

2.3.25 Question: How can systems thinking address the "fixes that fail" archetype?
Answer: By identifying and addressing root causes, systems thinking ensures sustainable solutions that prevent future problems.

Online Resources

More Practices Questions

Online Exam Paper
URL
https://forms.gle/57qZ5DPC5amtVx7z8

QR Code

YouTube Video Playlist Link
Chapter 2
URL
https://www.youtube.com/playlist?list=PLzlh_31VWEFqjZ8cTSljUPFe3jg_cuuQL

QR Code

Chapter 3: Requirement Analysis and Planning

3.1 Gathering User Requirements

3.1.1 Question: What is requirement analysis?
Answer: Requirement analysis is the process of determining user expectations for a new or modified product, detailing what the system should do.

3.1.2 Question: Why is requirement gathering important?
Answer: Requirement gathering is crucial because it ensures the system meets user needs and expectations, reducing the risk of project failure.

3.1.3 Question: What are the main techniques for gathering requirements?
Answer: Common techniques include interviews, surveys, questionnaires, focus groups, and observation.

3.1.4 Question: What is a stakeholder in the context of requirement gathering?
Answer: A stakeholder is anyone with an interest in the project, including end-users, customers, managers, and developers.

3.1.5 Question: How do you identify stakeholders?
Answer: Stakeholders can be identified through organizational charts, project documents, and consulting with project managers and team members.

3.1.6 Question: What is the purpose of an interview in requirement gathering?
Answer: Interviews are used to directly collect detailed information from stakeholders, clarifying their needs and expectations.

3.1.7 Question: What are some common questions to ask during a requirement gathering interview?
Answer: Questions typically cover the current system's functionality, desired improvements, user challenges, and specific needs.

3.1.8 Question: What is a focus group?
Answer: A focus group is a gathering of selected stakeholders to discuss and provide feedback on system requirements collectively.

3.1.9 Question: How does observation help in gathering requirements?
Answer: Observation involves watching how users interact with the current system to identify inefficiencies and areas for improvement.

3.1.10 Question: What is a requirement specification document?
Answer: It is a detailed description of the system's functional and non-functional requirements, serving as a reference for development.

3.1.11 Question: What is a use case in requirement gathering?
Answer: A use case describes a specific scenario in which the system interacts with users or other systems to achieve a goal.

3.1.12 Question: Why are use cases important?
Answer: Use cases help in understanding user interactions and system functionality, guiding the design and development process.

3.1.13 Question: What is a functional requirement?
Answer: Functional requirements specify what the system should do, detailing its features and capabilities.

3.1.14 Question: What is a non-functional requirement?

Answer: Non-functional requirements define the system's operational attributes, such as performance, usability, and security.

3.1.15 Question: What is the role of a systems analyst in requirement gathering?

Answer: A systems analyst facilitates requirement gathering, ensuring that stakeholder needs are accurately captured and documented.

3.1.16 Question: What are some challenges in requirement gathering?

Answer: Common challenges include ambiguous requirements, changing requirements, and communication barriers between stakeholders.

3.1.17 Question: What is a requirement validation?

Answer: Requirement validation involves checking that the gathered requirements accurately reflect the stakeholders' needs and are feasible to implement.

3.1.18 Question: How do you prioritize requirements?

Answer: Requirements can be prioritized based on factors such as stakeholder impact, feasibility, cost, and project timeline.

3.1.19 Question: What is a requirement traceability matrix?

Answer: It is a tool used to track requirements throughout the project lifecycle, ensuring that all requirements are addressed in the final system.

3.1.20 Question: What is prototyping in requirement gathering?

Answer: Prototyping involves creating an early model of the system to help stakeholders visualize requirements and provide feedback.

3.1.21 Question: What are the benefits of prototyping?

Answer: Benefits include early detection of issues, better user feedback, and clearer requirements definition.

3.1.22 Question: What is a JAD session?

Answer: Joint Application Development (JAD) is a collaborative workshop where stakeholders and developers work together to define requirements.

3.1.23 Question: What is the role of documentation in requirement gathering?

Answer: Documentation records the requirements, ensuring clarity and providing a reference for stakeholders and developers.

3.1.24 Question: How do you handle conflicting requirements?

Answer: Conflicting requirements are resolved through negotiation, prioritization, and sometimes compromise, ensuring the best overall outcome.

3.1.25 Question: What is a requirements elicitation?

Answer: Requirements elicitation is the process of collecting information from stakeholders to understand their needs and expectations for the system.

3.1.26 Question: What tools are commonly used in requirement gathering?

Answer: Common tools include document templates, requirement management software, diagramming tools, and collaboration platforms.

3.1.27 Question: What is a user story?

Answer: A user story is a simple, informal description of a feature told from the perspective of an end-user.

3.1.28 Question: What is the importance of user stories?

Answer: User stories help in capturing functional requirements in a user-centric way, facilitating better understanding and communication.

3.1.29 Question: What is requirement modelling?
Answer: Requirement modelling involves creating visual representations of requirements to help stakeholders and developers understand them better.

3.1.30 Question: How do you ensure requirements are complete?
Answer: Ensuring completeness involves thorough validation, stakeholder review, and cross-referencing with project objectives and constraints.

3.2 Analysing and Documenting Requirements

3.2.1 Question: What is requirement analysis?
Answer: Requirement analysis is the process of defining user expectations for a new or modified product, determining the needs and conditions to meet for a project's successful completion.

3.2.2 Question: Why is requirement analysis important?
Answer: It ensures that the system meets the needs of users and stakeholders, reducing the risk of project failure due to misunderstood or missing requirements.

3.2.3 Question: What are functional requirements?
Answer: Functional requirements specify what the system should do, describing its functionality, tasks, and behaviours.

3.2.4 Question: What are non-functional requirements?
Answer: Non-functional requirements define the system's operational attributes, such as performance, usability, reliability, and security.

3.2.5 Question: What is a requirement specification document?
Answer: A requirement specification document details the functional and non-functional requirements of a system, serving as a reference for developers and stakeholders.

3.2.6 Question: What is the difference between user requirements and system requirements?
Answer: User requirements describe what users need from the system, while system requirements detail how the system should be built to meet those needs.

3.2.7 Question: What are the steps involved in requirement analysis?
Answer: Steps include requirement gathering, requirement modelling, requirement validation, and documentation.

3.2.8 Question: What techniques are used for requirement gathering?
Answer: Techniques include interviews, surveys, questionnaires, observations, and workshops.

3.2.9 Question: What is a use case in requirement analysis?
Answer: A use case describes how a user interacts with the system to achieve a specific goal, capturing functional requirements.

3.2.10 Question: What is a stakeholder in the context of requirement analysis?
Answer: A stakeholder is anyone who has an interest in or is affected by the system, including users, clients, and developers.

3.2.11 Question: What is requirement validation?
Answer: Requirement validation ensures that the documented requirements accurately reflect the needs and expectations of stakeholders.

3.2.12 Question: What is a requirement traceability matrix?
Answer: A requirement traceability matrix links requirements to their origin and tracks them throughout the project lifecycle to ensure they are met.

3.2.13 Question: What is the role of a business analyst in requirement analysis?
Answer: A business analyst bridges the gap between stakeholders and developers, ensuring requirements are clearly understood and documented.

3.2.14 Question: What is the difference between requirements elicitation and requirements analysis?
Answer: Requirements elicitation involves gathering requirements from stakeholders, while requirements analysis involves refining, modelling, and documenting these requirements.

3.2.15 Question: What is scope creep?
Answer: Scope creep refers to uncontrolled changes or additions to the project scope without corresponding adjustments in time, cost, and resources.

3.2.16 Question: How can you prevent scope creep?
Answer: Prevent scope creep by clearly defining requirements, documenting all changes, and obtaining formal approval for changes.

3.2.17 Question: What is a functional specification?
Answer: A functional specification details the functionality of the system, including inputs, outputs, and processing logic.

3.2.18 Question: What is a non-functional specification?
Answer: A non-functional specification defines system attributes like performance, usability, reliability, and security.

3.2.19 Question: What is the importance of documenting requirements?
Answer: Documenting requirements ensures a clear understanding of the system's needs, provides a reference for development, and helps manage changes.

3.2.20 Question: What is requirements prioritization?
Answer: Requirements prioritization involves ranking requirements based on their importance and urgency to ensure critical features are developed first.

3.2.21 Question: What are the common challenges in requirement analysis?
Answer: Challenges include unclear requirements, changing requirements, communication gaps, and conflicting stakeholder interests.

3.2.22 Question: What is the role of prototyping in requirement analysis?
Answer: Prototyping helps validate requirements by creating an early model of the system, allowing stakeholders to provide feedback.

3.2.23 Question: What is the difference between functional and non-functional requirements?
Answer: Functional requirements describe what the system should do, while non-functional requirements describe how the system performs its functions.

3.2.24 Question: What is a requirements management plan?
Answer: A requirements management plan outlines how requirements will be identified, documented, tracked, and managed throughout the project.

3.2.25 Question: What is the purpose of requirement modelling?
Answer: Requirement modelling visualizes and refines requirements, helping stakeholders understand and validate them.

3.2.26 Question: What is a requirement elicitation technique?
Answer: Techniques like interviews, surveys, and workshops gather detailed requirements from stakeholders.

3.2.27 Question: What is the role of use cases in documenting requirements?
Answer: Use cases capture functional requirements by describing user interactions with the system to achieve specific goals.

3.2.28 Question: How do you handle conflicting requirements?
Answer: Handle conflicting requirements by prioritizing them, negotiating with stakeholders, and finding a compromise that aligns with project goals.

3.2.29 Question: What is a requirement baseline?
Answer: A requirement baseline is a set of approved requirements that serves as a basis for further development and changes.

3.2.30 Question: What is requirements verification?
Answer: Requirements verification ensures that requirements are correctly implemented in the system, meeting stakeholder needs.

3.2.31 Question: How do you manage changes to requirements?
Answer: Manage changes by documenting them, assessing their impact, and obtaining formal approval before implementation.

3.2.32 Question: What is a context diagram?
Answer: A context diagram shows the system's boundaries, external entities interacting with the system, and data flows between them.

3.2.33 Question: What is requirements traceability?
Answer: Requirements traceability tracks the origin and fulfilment of each requirement throughout the project lifecycle.

3.2.34 Question: What is a user story in Agile methodology?
Answer: A user story is a brief description of a feature from the perspective of an end-user, capturing functional requirements.

3.2.35 Question: What is a requirements workshop?
Answer: A requirements workshop is a collaborative session where stakeholders discuss and define requirements.

3.2.36 Question: How do you validate requirements?
Answer: Validate requirements by reviewing them with stakeholders, prototyping, and testing to ensure they meet the intended needs.

3.2.37 Question: What is requirements analysis and specification?
Answer: It involves refining gathered requirements and documenting them in a detailed specification for development.

3.2.38 Question: What is the importance of stakeholder engagement in requirement analysis?
Answer: Engaging stakeholders ensures their needs are understood and incorporated into the system, improving project success.

3.2.39 Question: What is a data dictionary?
Answer: A data dictionary is a repository that defines data elements, their meanings, and relationships in a system.

3.2.40 Question: How do you ensure requirement completeness?

Answer: Ensure completeness by thoroughly reviewing requirements, cross-referencing with stakeholder needs, and validating through prototypes and tests.

3.3 Managing Requirements Changes

3.3.1 Question: What is requirements change management?
Answer: Requirements change management is the process of handling changes to system requirements during the development lifecycle, ensuring all changes are systematically evaluated and documented.

3.3.2 Question: Why is managing requirements changes important?
Answer: Managing requirements changes is crucial to maintain project scope, schedule, and budget while ensuring the final system meets user needs and adapts to evolving requirements.

3.3.3 Question: What are common causes of requirements changes?
Answer: Common causes include changes in business processes, market conditions, regulatory requirements, stakeholder feedback, and technical advancements.

3.3.4 Question: What is a change request?
Answer: A change request is a formal proposal for an alteration to the system requirements, submitted for evaluation and approval by the project stakeholders.

3.3.5 Question: How do you assess the impact of a requirements change?
Answer: Assessing the impact involves analysing how the change affects the system's functionality, performance, schedule, cost, and risk, and evaluating its feasibility.

3.3.6 Question: What is a change control board (CCB)?
Answer: A change control board is a group of stakeholders responsible for reviewing, evaluating, and approving or rejecting change requests in a project.

3.3.7 Question: What is the role of a systems analyst in managing requirements changes?
Answer: A systems analyst evaluates the impact of proposed changes, communicates with stakeholders, updates documentation, and ensures changes are implemented correctly.

3.3.8 Question: What tools are commonly used for managing requirements changes?
Answer: Common tools include requirement management software like JIRA, IBM Rational DOORS, and Microsoft Azure DevOps, which help track changes and maintain documentation.

3.3.9 Question: What is traceability in requirements management?
Answer: Traceability ensures that each requirement can be traced back to its origin, such as business objectives, stakeholder needs, or regulatory requirements, throughout the project lifecycle.

3.3.10 Question: How do you maintain traceability when requirements change?
Answer: Maintaining traceability involves updating traceability matrices, linking changes to specific requirements, and documenting the rationale and impact of each change.

3.3.11 Question: What is a baseline in requirements management?
Answer: A baseline is a fixed reference point representing the agreed-upon requirements at a specific time, against which changes can be measured and managed.

3.3.12 Question: How do you handle conflicting requirements during changes?
Answer: Handling conflicts involves prioritizing requirements based on business value, engaging stakeholders to resolve disagreements, and finding compromise solutions.

3.3.13 Question: What is the significance of communication in managing requirements changes?
Answer: Effective communication ensures all stakeholders are aware of changes, understand their impact, and agree on the implementation approach, reducing misunderstandings and resistance.

3.3.14 Question: What is a requirements change log?
Answer: Requirements change log is a document that records all change requests, including their status, impact assessment, approval, and implementation details.

3.3.15 Question: How do you prioritize change requests?
Answer: Change requests are prioritized based on factors such as business value, urgency, impact on project goals, and available resources.

3.3.16 Question: What are the challenges of managing requirements changes?
Answer: Challenges include scope creep, maintaining documentation accuracy, balancing stakeholder interests, and managing the impact on project timelines and budgets.

3.3.17 Question: What is scope creep?
Answer: Scope creep refers to the uncontrolled expansion of project scope without corresponding changes to time, cost, and resources, often due to unapproved requirement changes.

3.3.18 Question: How can you prevent scope creep?
Answer: Preventing scope creep involves strict change control processes, clear documentation, stakeholder agreement, and continuous monitoring of project scope.

3.3.19 Question: What is a rollback plan in requirements management?
Answer: A rollback plan outlines steps to revert to a previous state if a change is found to be infeasible or causes issues, ensuring minimal disruption to the project.

3.3.20 Question: How do you document requirements change?
Answer: Documenting a change involves updating requirement specifications, traceability matrices, impact assessments, and ensuring all relevant documents reflect the new requirements.

3.3.21 Question: What is version control in requirements management?
Answer: Version control is the process of managing different versions of requirements documents to track changes, maintain history, and ensure stakeholders are using the correct versions.

3.3.22 Question: How do you ensure stakeholder alignment on requirements changes?
Answer: Ensuring alignment involves regular communication, involving stakeholders in the change control process, and obtaining formal approvals for changes.

3.3.23 Question: What is the role of user acceptance testing (UAT) in managing requirements changes?
Answer: UAT ensures that changes meet user needs and work as intended, providing final validation before the changes are deployed to the production environment.

3.3.24 Question: How do you manage changes in an Agile environment?
Answer: In Agile, changes are managed through iterative development, regular feedback loops, flexible planning, and prioritizing changes in the product backlog.

3.3.25 Question: What is continuous improvement in requirements management?
Answer: Continuous improvement involves regularly evaluating and refining processes for managing requirements changes to enhance efficiency, quality, and stakeholder satisfaction.

3.3.26 Question: How do you handle changes that impact project deadlines?
Answer: Handling such changes involves reassessing project schedules, negotiating new deadlines, reallocating resources, and communicating impacts to stakeholders.

3.3.27 Question: What is the importance of stakeholder feedback in managing requirements changes?
Answer: Stakeholder feedback ensures that changes align with user needs and expectations, improving the likelihood of project success and stakeholder satisfaction.

3.3.28 Question: How do you measure the success of requirements change management?
Answer: Success can be measured through metrics such as the number of successfully implemented changes, stakeholder satisfaction, adherence to schedule and budget, and quality improvements.

3.3.29 Question: What is impact analysis in the context of requirements changes?
Answer: Impact analysis assesses the potential effects of a change on the system, including technical, functional, and business aspects, helping to make informed decisions.

3.3.30 Question: How do you train team members on managing requirements changes?
Answer: Training involves educating team members on change control processes, tools, documentation standards, and the importance of communication and collaboration.

3.3.31 Question: What is the role of documentation in managing requirements changes?
Answer: Documentation provides a clear, traceable record of all changes, supporting communication, decision-making, and ensuring that the project stays aligned with its goals.

3.3.32 Question: How do you manage urgent requirements changes?
Answer: Managing urgent changes involves expediting the evaluation and approval process, clearly communicating the urgency and impact, and prioritizing implementation.

3.3.33 Question: What is a change impact matrix?
Answer: A change impact matrix is a tool used to visualize the potential effects of a change on different parts of the system, aiding in comprehensive impact analysis.

3.3.34 Question: How do you handle rejected change requests?
Answer: Rejected change requests should be documented with reasons for rejection, and the decision communicated to stakeholders to ensure transparency and understanding.

3.3.35 Question: What is the significance of stakeholder buy-in for requirements changes?
Answer: Stakeholder buy-in ensures support and cooperation for implementing changes, reducing resistance and increasing the likelihood of successful adoption.

3.3.36 Question: How do you ensure changes are aligned with business objectives?
Answer: Ensuring alignment involves evaluating changes against business goals, involving key stakeholders in decision-making, and regularly reviewing project objectives.

3.3.37 Question: What is requirements volatility?
Answer: Requirements volatility refers to the frequency and extent of changes to requirements during the project lifecycle, which can impact project stability and outcomes.

3.3.38 Question: How can you mitigate the effects of high requirements volatility?
Answer: Mitigating effects involves using flexible development methodologies, maintaining open communication with stakeholders, and implementing robust change control processes.

3.3.39 Question: What is the role of negotiation in managing requirements changes?
Answer: Negotiation helps resolve conflicts, align stakeholder interests, and find mutually acceptable solutions for implementing changes without compromising project goals.

3.3.40 Question: How do you handle changes that impact project budget?
Answer: Handling such changes involves reassessing the budget, exploring alternative solutions, negotiating additional funding if necessary, and communicating impacts to stakeholders.

Online Resources

More Practices Questions

Online Exam Paper

URL

https://forms.gle/Pe4amtp3LjoHcg777

QR Code

YouTube Video Playlist Link

Chapter 3

URL https://www.youtube.com/playlist?list=PLzlh_31VWEFqKDjSxp4-STfqxQf95Np5D

QR Code

Chapter 4: System Modelling

4.1 Overview of System Modelling

4.1.1 Question: What is system modelling?
Answer: System modelling involves creating abstract representations of a system to understand and communicate its structure and behaviour.

4.1.2 Question: Why is system modelling important?
Answer: System modelling is crucial as it helps in visualizing, analysing, and documenting a system's structure and operations, facilitating better design and communication among stakeholders.

4.1.3 Question: What are the common types of system models?
Answer: Common types include data flow diagrams (DFD), entity-relationship diagrams (ERD), use case diagrams, class diagrams, and sequence diagrams.

4.1.4 Question: What is a Data Flow Diagram (DFD)?
Answer: A DFD is a graphical representation of data processes, data flow, and data storage within a system.

4.1.5 Question: What is the purpose of a Context Diagram?
Answer: A context diagram shows the system boundaries, external entities that interact with the system, and the main data flows between them.

4.1.6 Question: What are the levels of DFD?
Answer: Levels of DFD include Level 0 (context diagram) and more detailed levels (Level 1, 2, etc.) which break down processes further.

4.1.7 Question: What is an Entity-Relationship Diagram (ERD)?
Answer: An ERD represents entities in a system and their relationships, primarily used in database design.

4.1.8 Question: What is a use case diagram?
Answer: A use case diagram is a UML diagram that depicts the interactions between users (actors) and a system to show functional requirements.

4.1.9 Question: What is a class diagram in UML?
Answer: A class diagram shows the static structure of a system, including classes, their attributes, operations, and relationships.

4.1.10 Question: What is a sequence diagram in UML?
Answer: A sequence diagram shows object interactions arranged in a time sequence, detailing the messages exchanged between objects.

4.1.11 Question: What is the role of a systems analyst in system modelling?
Answer: A systems analyst creates models to represent the system's requirements and design, ensuring that the final system meets user needs and functions correctly.

4.1.12 Question: What is object-oriented modelling?
Answer: Object-oriented modelling uses objects and classes to represent and design a system, emphasizing reuse and modularity.

4.1.13 Question: What is the difference between logical and physical models?
Answer: Logical models represent what the system must do, while physical models describe how the system will be implemented.

4.1.14 Question: What are the benefits of using UML for system modelling?

Answer: UML provides a standardized way to visualize system design, improves communication among stakeholders, and supports documentation and analysis.

4.1.15 Question: What is the importance of modelling tools in system design?
Answer: Modelling tools facilitate the creation, visualization, and analysis of system models, improving accuracy and efficiency in system design.

4.1.16 Question: What is a state diagram in UML?
Answer: A state diagram shows the states of an object and the transitions between those states in response to events.

4.1.17 Question: What is the purpose of activity diagrams?
Answer: Activity diagrams depict the flow of control or data within a system, illustrating the sequence of activities and their dependencies.

4.1.18 Question: How does system modelling aid in requirement validation?
Answer: System modelling helps validate requirements by providing a visual representation of the system, ensuring all requirements are captured and correctly understood.

4.1.19 Question: What is a component diagram in UML?
Answer: A component diagram shows the organization and dependencies among software components, illustrating how a system is divided into components and their interactions.

4.1.20 Question: What is a deployment diagram in UML?
Answer: A deployment diagram depicts the physical deployment of artifacts on nodes, showing how software and hardware components interact.

4.1.21 Question: What is a package diagram in UML?
Answer: A package diagram organizes classes and other elements into packages, representing the high-level structure of the system.

4.1.22 Question: What is the significance of use case scenarios?
Answer: Use case scenarios describe specific sequences of actions or events in a use case, helping to clarify requirements and design decisions.

4.1.23 Question: What is the purpose of a flowchart?
Answer: A flowchart represents the sequence of steps in a process or system, using symbols and arrows to illustrate the flow of control.

4.1.24 Question: How do models support system integration?
Answer: Models provide a detailed blueprint of system components and their interactions, facilitating the integration process by ensuring compatibility and coherence.

4.1.25 Question: What is a collaboration diagram in UML?
Answer: A collaboration diagram shows interactions between objects and their relationships, emphasizing the structural organization of the system.

4.1.26 Question: What is a use case narrative?
Answer: A use case narrative is a detailed textual description of a use case, outlining the interactions between actors and the system.

4.1.27 Question: How do ERDs aid in database design?
Answer: ERDs help in visualizing the data structure, defining entities, attributes, and relationships, which is crucial for designing an efficient database schema.

4.1.28 Question: What is the role of abstraction in system modelling?

Answer: Abstraction simplifies complex systems by focusing on essential details, making it easier to understand, design, and communicate the system.

4.1.29 Question: What is a boundary in system modelling?
Answer: A boundary defines the limits of a system, distinguishing between what is inside and outside the system.

4.1.30 Question: What is the importance of feedback in system models?
Answer: Feedback mechanisms in system models help in identifying errors and improving the system through iterative refinement and validation.

4.1.31 Question: What is a subsystem in system modelling?
Answer: A subsystem is a self-contained module within a larger system, which can be developed and analysed independently but interacts with other subsystems.

4.1.32 Question: How does modelling support system documentation?
Answer: Modelling provides detailed diagrams and descriptions that serve as comprehensive documentation for system design, development, and maintenance.

4.1.33 Question: What is the importance of scenario-based modelling?
Answer: Scenario-based modelling captures different usage scenarios of a system, helping to identify and design for various user interactions and edge cases.

4.1.34 Question: What is a swimlane diagram?
Answer: A swimlane diagram is a type of flowchart that divides the process steps into lanes, each representing a different actor or part of the system, clarifying responsibilities and interactions.

4.1.35 Question: What is the significance of modularity in system design?
Answer: Modularity divides a system into smaller, manageable components or modules, promoting reuse, maintainability, and parallel development.

4.2 Use Case Modelling

4.2.1 Question: What is use case modelling?
Answer: Use case modelling is a technique used in system analysis to identify, clarify, and organize system requirements. It involves creating use case diagrams to represent interactions between users and the system.

4.2.2 Question: What is a use case?
Answer: A use case is a description of a system's behaviour as it responds to a request from an actor or another system, detailing the interactions to achieve a specific goal.

4.2.3 Question: Who is an actor in use case modelling?
Answer: An actor represents a role played by a user or any other system that interacts with the subject (system) to achieve a use case.

4.2.4 Question: What is the purpose of a use case diagram?
Answer: The purpose of a use case diagram is to provide a high-level visual representation of the system's functional requirements, illustrating how users interact with the system.

4.2.5 Question: What are the key elements of a use case diagram?
Answer: The key elements include actors, use cases, system boundary, and relationships (associations, generalizations, and include/extend relationships).

4.2.6 Question: What is the system boundary in use case modelling?
Answer: The system boundary defines the scope of the system, showing what is inside and outside the system, typically represented by a rectangle in a use case diagram.

4.2.7 Question: Can you explain the "include" relationship in use case diagrams?
Answer: The "include" relationship indicates that a use case contains the behaviour of another use case as part of its execution, promoting reuse and modularity.

4.2.8 Question: What is the "extend" relationship in use case diagrams?
Answer: The "extend" relationship shows that a use case can be extended with additional behaviour under certain conditions, providing optional functionality.

4.2.9 Question: How do you identify use cases?
Answer: Use cases are identified by analysinguser requirements, business processes, and scenarios where users interact with the system to achieve specific goals.

4.2.10 Question: What is a primary actor in use case modelling?
Answer: A primary actor is the main user that initiates an interaction with the system to achieve a goal or complete a task.

4.2.11 Question: What is a secondary actor in use case modelling?
Answer: A secondary actor assists the primary actor or the system in achieving the use case goals, often representing external systems or roles.

4.2.12 Question: What is a use case specification?
Answer: A use case specification is a detailed textual description of a use case, outlining the preconditions, postconditions, flow of events, and exceptions.

4.2.13 Question: Why are use case diagrams important in system analysis?
Answer: Use case diagrams help in understanding system requirements, identifying user interactions, and communicating functionality to stakeholders.

4.2.14 Question: What is the difference between a use case and a user story?
Answer: A use case is a detailed interaction between users and the system, while a user story is a short, simple description of a feature from the user's perspective.

4.2.15 Question: What is a precondition in a use case specification?
Answer: A precondition is a condition that must be true before a use case can begin, ensuring the system is in a specific state.

4.2.16 Question: What is a postcondition in a use case specification?
Answer: A postcondition is a condition that must be true after the use case has been executed, ensuring the system reaches a specific state.

4.2.17 Question: What is an alternative flow in a use case?
Answer: An alternative flow describes variations in the use case that occur under specific conditions, deviating from the main success path.

4.2.18 Question: What is the main success scenario in a use case?
Answer: The main success scenario outlines the primary, straightforward sequence of events leading to the successful completion of the use case.

4.2.19 Question: How do use cases support requirements management?
Answer: Use cases help in organizing and managing functional requirements, ensuring all interactions are captured and traced throughout the development process.

4.2.20 Question: What is an exception flow in a use case?
Answer: An exception flow describes the sequence of events that occurs when an error or unexpected condition arises during the execution of a use case.

4.2.21 Question: How do use cases improve communication with stakeholders?
Answer: Use cases provide a clear and structured way to describe system functionality, making it easier for stakeholders to understand and validate requirements.

4.2.22 Question: What is the relationship between use cases and system testing?
Answer: Use cases are used to derive test cases, ensuring that all user interactions and requirements are validated through testing.

4.2.23 Question: What is the role of use case diagrams in project documentation?
Answer: Use case diagrams serve as a visual reference in project documentation, providing a concise overview of system interactions and requirements.

4.2.24 Question: How do you handle complex use cases?
Answer: Complex use cases can be managed by breaking them down into smaller, more manageable sub-use cases or by using include and extend relationships.

4.2.25 Question: What is the importance of actors' roles in use case diagrams?
Answer: Actors' roles help in identifying the different users and systems that interact with the system, ensuring all perspectives are considered in the design.

4.2.26 Question: How do you prioritize use cases?
Answer: Use cases are prioritized based on factors such as business value, risk, and dependency, ensuring critical functionalities are addressed first.

4.2.27 Question: Can use cases be used in Agile development?
Answer: Yes, use cases can be adapted for Agile development, providing a structured approach to capturing requirements and guiding iterative development.

4.2.28 Question: What tools are commonly used for creating use case diagrams?
Answer: Common tools include UML diagramming tools like Microsoft Visio, Lucidchart, Enterprise Architect, and online tools like Draw.io.

4.2.29 Question: How do use cases relate to user experience (UX) design?
Answer: Use cases help UX designers understand user goals and interactions, informing the design of intuitive and user-friendly interfaces.

4.2.30 Question: What is a use case scenario?
Answer: A use case scenario is a detailed narrative that describes a specific instance of a use case, showing how the system and actors interact in a particular situation.

4.3 Activity Diagrams

4.3.1 Question: What is an activity diagram?
Answer: An activity diagram is a UML behavioural diagram that represents the flow of activities within a system, showing the sequence and conditions for coordinating lower-level behaviours.

4.3.2 Question: What are the key elements of an activity diagram?
Answer: Key elements include activities, transitions, decisions, merges, forks, joins, swimlanes, and start and end nodes.

4.3.3 Question: What is the purpose of an activity diagram?
Answer: The purpose is to model the dynamic aspects of a system, visualize workflows, and understand the sequence of activities and their dependencies.

4.3.4 Question: How do you represent the start of a process in an activity diagram?

Answer: The start of a process is represented by a filled circle, also known as the initial node.

4.3.5 Question: How do you represent the end of a process in an activity diagram?
Answer: The end of a process is represented by a filled circle with a border, known as the final node.

4.3.6 Question: What is a decision node in an activity diagram?
Answer: A decision node is a diamond-shaped symbol that represents a branching point where the flow can take different paths based on conditions.

4.3.7 Question: What is a merge node in an activity diagram?
Answer: A merge node is a diamond-shaped symbol that brings multiple alternate flows together into a single flow.

4.3.8 Question: What is a fork node in an activity diagram?
Answer: A fork node is a bar that splits a single flow into multiple concurrent flows.

4.3.9 Question: What is a join node in an activity diagram?
Answer: A join node is a bar that synchronizes multiple concurrent flows into a single flow.

4.3.10 Question: What are Swimlanes in an activity diagram?
Answer: Swimlanes are partitions that divide activities based on the responsibilities of different actors or system components.

4.3.11 Question: How do you depict an activity in an activity diagram?
Answer: An activity is depicted as a rounded rectangle containing the name of the activity.

4.3.12 Question: What is the role of transitions in an activity diagram?
Answer: Transitions are arrows that represent the flow of control or data between activities.

4.3.13 Question: What is the difference between a control flow and an object flow in an activity diagram?
Answer: A control flow represents the sequence of execution, while an object flow shows the movement of objects between activities.

4.3.14 Question: Can you explain the use of guard conditions in activity diagrams?
Answer: Guard conditions are Boolean expressions on transitions that must be true for the flow to proceed.

4.3.15 Question: What is an interruptible activity region?
Answer: An interruptible activity region is a dashed boundary that contains activities which can be interrupted by events or conditions.

4.3.16 Question: How do activity diagrams differ from flowcharts?
Answer: Activity diagrams are more detailed, supporting concurrent flows, complex decision-making, and the depiction of object flows, while flowcharts are simpler and primarily linear.

4.3.17 Question: What is the significance of using activity diagrams in system design?
Answer: Activity diagrams help in understanding the workflow and identifying potential bottlenecks, improving system efficiency and clarity.

4.3.18 Question: What is the use of expansion regions in activity diagrams?
Answer: Expansion regions represent a set of activities that are repeated for each item in a collection, showing iterative or parallel processing.

4.3.19 Question: How can activity diagrams be used in business process modelling?
Answer: They can model business processes by depicting the sequence of activities, roles involved, and decision points, aiding in process optimization.

4.3.20 Question: What is an activity partition?
Answer: An activity partition, also known as a swimlane, organizes activities into groups based on responsibilities or roles.

4.3.21 Question: How do you represent concurrent activities in an activity diagram?
Answer: Concurrent activities are represented using fork and join nodes, allowing multiple activities to execute simultaneously.

4.3.22 Question: What is the role of an action in an activity diagram?
Answer: An action is the smallest unit of behaviour, representing a single step within an activity.

4.3.23 Question: How do you handle exceptions in activity diagrams?
Answer: Exceptions are handled using interruptible activity regions and exception handlers, showing how the flow is redirected in case of errors.

4.3.24 Question: What is a sub activity in an activity diagram?
Answer: A sub activity is an activity that is part of a larger activity, allowing complex activities to be broken down into manageable parts.

4.3.25 Question: How do activity diagrams facilitate communication among stakeholders?
Answer: They provide a clear visual representation of workflows, making it easier for stakeholders to understand and discuss processes.

4.3.26 Question: What is the role of tokens in activity diagrams?
Answer: Tokens are abstract markers that indicate the progress of control and object flows within the diagram.

4.3.27 Question: How do you model time events in an activity diagram?
Answer: Time events are modelled using clocks and time constraints, indicating when certain activities should start or end.

4.3.28 Question: What is a flow final node?
Answer: A flow final node is a small circle with an "X" inside, indicating the end of a specific flow path without terminating the entire activity.

4.3.29 Question: How do you represent input and output pins in activity diagrams?
Answer: Input and output pins are small rectangles attached to actions, showing where data enters and exits an activity.

4.3.30 Question: What is the use of activity diagrams in software engineering?
Answer: They are used to model the workflow of system processes, identify interactions, and ensure that all possible scenarios are considered.

4.3.31 Question: How can activity diagrams help in system testing?
Answer: They help identify all possible execution paths, ensuring comprehensive test coverage and highlighting potential issues.

4.3.32 Question: What is a central buffer node in an activity diagram?
Answer: A central buffer node is used to store data temporarily, managing the flow of objects between activities.

4.3.33 Question: How do activity diagrams support the Agile methodology?
Answer: They provide a clear, iterative view of workflows, supporting continuous development and collaboration.

4.3.34 Question: What is an initial node in an activity diagram?
Answer: An initial node represents the starting point of an activity, depicted as a filled black circle.

4.3.35 Question: How do you model complex decision-making processes in activity diagrams?
Answer: Complex decisions are modelled using multiple decision and merge nodes, along with guard conditions to manage the flow.

4.4 Entity-Relationship Diagrams

4.4.1 Question: What is an Entity-Relationship Diagram (ERD)?
Answer: An ERD is a graphical representation of entities and their relationships in a database, used for data modelling and database design.

4.4.2 Question: What are entities in ERD?
Answer: Entities are objects or things in the real world that have a distinct existence, represented as rectangles in ERD.

4.4.3 Question: What are attributes in ERD?
Answer: Attributes are properties or characteristics of entities, represented as ovals connected to their respective entities.

4.4.4 Question: What are relationships in ERD?
Answer: Relationships represent associations between entities, depicted as diamonds connected to the involved entities.

4.4.5 Question: What is a primary key in ERD?
Answer: A primary key is a unique identifier for an entity, ensuring that each entity instance can be uniquely identified.

4.4.6 Question: What is a foreign key in ERD?
Answer: A foreign key is an attribute that creates a link between two entities, pointing to the primary key of another entity.

4.4.7 Question: Can you explain the concept of cardinality in ERD?
Answer: Cardinality specifies the number of instances of one entity that can be associated with instances of another entity, such as one-to-one, one-to-many, or many-to-many.

4.4.8 Question: What is a weak entity in ERD?
Answer: A weak entity is an entity that cannot be uniquely identified by its attributes alone and relies on a strong entity, usually connected by a double rectangle.

4.4.9 Question: What is a composite attribute in ERD?
Answer: A composite attribute is an attribute that can be divided into smaller sub-parts, each representing more basic attributes.

4.4.10 Question: What is a derived attribute in ERD?
Answer: A derived attribute is an attribute whose value can be calculated from other attributes in the database.

4.4.11 Question: How are multi-valued attributes represented in ERD?
Answer: Multi-valued attributes, which can have multiple values, are represented by double ovals connected to their entities.

4.4.12 Question: What is the purpose of ERD in database design?
Answer: ERDs help in visualizing the data structure, identifying relationships, and ensuring a logical organization of data, which aids in effective database design.

4.4.13 Question: What is a ternary relationship in ERD?

Answer: A ternary relationship is a relationship that involves three entities, indicating an association among three different entities.

4.4.14 Question: What is a recursive relationship in ERD?
Answer: A recursive relationship is a relationship between instances of the same entity, where an entity has a relationship with itself.

4.4.15 Question: What is normalization in the context of ERD?
Answer: Normalization is the process of organizing data to reduce redundancy and improve data integrity, often visualized using ERDs.

4.4.16 Question: How do you represent a relationship with attributes in ERD?
Answer: Attributes of relationships are represented by ovals connected to the diamond symbol of the relationship.

4.4.17 Question: What is the difference between an entity and an attribute?
Answer: An entity is an object that exists independently, while an attribute is a property that describes an entity.

4.4.18 Question: How do you depict a many-to-many relationship in ERD?
Answer: A many-to-many relationship is depicted by connecting two entities with a diamond, indicating multiple instances of one entity can be associated with multiple instances of another entity.

4.4.19 Question: What is the significance of a composite key in ERD?
Answer: A composite key is a combination of two or more attributes that together uniquely identify an entity instance.

4.4.20 Question: What are identifying and non-identifying relationships in ERD?
Answer: Identifying relationships link weak entities to strong entities, forming part of the primary key, while non-identifying relationships do not affect the primary key.

4.4.21 Question: What is a super key in ERD?
Answer: A super key is a set of one or more attributes that can uniquely identify an entity instance in a relation.

4.4.22 Question: What is a candidate key in ERD?
Answer: A candidate key is a minimal super key, meaning it has no unnecessary attributes, and any of its subsets are not super keys.

4.4.23 Question: What is an associative entity in ERD?
Answer: An associative entity is used to convert a many-to-many relationship into two one-to-many relationships, often containing attributes that pertain to the relationship.

4.4.24 Question: How do you represent optionality in ERD?
Answer: Optionality is represented by using a circle (optional) or a line (mandatory) near the cardinality symbols on the relationship lines.

4.4.25 Question: What is the role of ERD in system analysis?
Answer: ERDs play a crucial role in system analysis by providing a clear and organized visualization of the data model, facilitating better understanding and communication among stakeholders.

4.4.26 Question: Can you explain the difference between logical and physical ERD?
Answer: A logical ERD focuses on the business and data requirements, while a physical ERD translates these into technical specifications for database creation.

4.4.27 Question: What is an entity set in ERD?

Answer: An entity set is a collection of similar entities that share the same attributes, representing a table in the database.

4.4.28 Question: How do you handle inheritance in ERD?
Answer: Inheritance in ERD is handled by creating a superclass for shared attributes and subclasses for specific attributes, connected with a generalization symbol.

4.4.29 Question: What is the purpose of ERD in the software development lifecycle?
Answer: ERDs are used in the design phase of the software development lifecycle to create a clear and structured blueprint of the database, aiding in efficient implementation and maintenance.

4.4.30 Question: How do you represent a one-to-one relationship in ERD?
Answer: A one-to-one relationship is represented by a line connecting two entities, each with a single cardinality symbol (1:1).

4.4.31 Question: What is the significance of a unique constraint in ERD?
Answer: A unique constraint ensures that all values in a column or a set of columns are distinct, preventing duplicate entries.

4.4.32 Question: What is the difference between an ERD and a class diagram?
Answer: An ERD focuses on data modelling and relationships between data entities, while a class diagram focuses on the structure and behaviour of classes and their relationships in object-oriented design.

4.4.33 Question: What are subtypes and supertypes in ERD?
Answer: Subtypes and supertypes represent hierarchical relationships where subtypes inherit attributes from supertypes, allowing for specialization and generalization.

4.4.34 Question: How do you ensure data integrity using ERD?
Answer: Data integrity is ensured by defining primary and foreign keys, constraints, and relationships in ERD, maintaining accurate and consistent data.

4.4.35 Question: What is the role of ERD in database normalization?
Answer: ERDs help visualize and organize data to eliminate redundancy and dependencies, facilitating the normalization process to achieve a well-structured database design.

4.5 Data Flow Diagrams

4.5.1 Question: What is a Data Flow Diagram (DFD)?
Answer: A DFD is a graphical representation of the flow of data through a system, showing how data is processed by the system in terms of inputs and outputs.

4.5.2 Question: What are the main components of a DFD?
Answer: The main components of a DFD are processes, data stores, data flows, and external entities.

4.5.3 Question: What does a process represent in a DFD?
Answer: A process represents a function or activity that transforms inputs into outputs within a system.

4.5.4 Question: What is a data store in a DFD?
Answer: A data store represents where data is stored within the system, such as a database or a file.

4.5.5 Question: What is an external entity in a DFD?
Answer: An external entity represents a source or destination of data outside the system being modelled, such as a user or another system.

4.5.6 Question: What is a data flow in a DFD?
Answer: A data flow represents the movement of data between processes, data stores, and external entities.

4.5.7 Question: What is the difference between a Level 0 and Level 1 DFD?
Answer: A Level 0 DFD, or context diagram, shows the system as a whole with its interactions with external entities. A Level 1 DFD breaks down the high-level process into sub-processes.

4.5.8 Question: What is a context diagram?
Answer: A context diagram is a high-level DFD that represents the system's boundaries and interactions with external entities, providing an overview of the system.

4.5.9 Question: Why is a context diagram important?
Answer: A context diagram provides a simplified view of the system, helping stakeholders understand the system's scope and interactions with external entities.

4.5.10 Question: What is the purpose of levelling in DFDs?
Answer: Levelling in DFDs breaks down processes into more detailed sub-processes, providing a clearer and more detailed view of the system's data flow.

4.5.11 Question: What are balancing DFDs?
Answer: Balancing DFDs ensure that data flow input and output remain consistent when moving from a higher-level DFD to a more detailed one.

4.5.12 Question: How do you ensure a DFD is accurate?
Answer: To ensure accuracy, validate the DFD against system requirements, review with stakeholders, and ensure consistency between different levels of DFDs.

4.5.13 Question: What is the role of a data dictionary in DFDs?
Answer: A data dictionary provides detailed information about data elements in a DFD, ensuring clarity and consistency in data definitions.

4.5.14 Question: How do you represent a data store in a DFD?
Answer: A data store in a DFD is represented by two parallel lines or an open-ended rectangle, indicating where data is stored.

4.5.15 Question: How do you represent a process in a DFD?
Answer: A process in a DFD is represented by a circle or a rounded rectangle, indicating a transformation of data.

4.5.16 Question: How do you represent an external entity in a DFD?
Answer: An external entity in a DFD is represented by a rectangle, indicating a source or destination of data outside the system.

4.5.17 Question: What are the rules for naming processes in a DFD?
Answer: Processes should be named using verb-noun phrases to clearly describe the action, such as "Process Orders" or "Generate Report."

4.5.18 Question: What are the common errors in DFDs?
Answer: Common errors include data flow loops, missing data flows, unbalanced DFD levels, and incorrect process naming.

4.5.19 Question: How do you handle complex processes in a DFD?
Answer: Complex processes can be broken down into sub-processes using levelling, creating more detailed DFDs to simplify and clarify the system.

4.5.20 Question: What is a logical DFD?
Answer: A logical DFD focuses on the business and data requirements, representing what the system must do without detailing how it will be implemented.

4.5.21 Question: What is a physical DFD?
Answer: A physical DFD shows how the system will be implemented, including hardware, software, files, and people involved in the processes.

4.5.22 Question: What are the benefits of using DFDs?
Answer: Benefits of DFDs include improved understanding of the system, identification of inefficiencies, and effective communication among stakeholders.

4.5.23 Question: How do DFDs help in system design?
Answer: DFDs help in system design by providing a clear and structured representation of data flows, making it easier to identify requirements and design solutions.

4.5.24 Question: What is the difference between a DFD and a flowchart?
Answer: A DFD focuses on the flow of data through a system, while a flowchart illustrates the flow of control or sequence of activities.

4.5.25 Question: How do you validate a DFD?
Answer: Validate a DFD by checking for logical consistency, ensuring all data flows are represented, and reviewing with stakeholders for accuracy.

4.5.26 Question: What is data partitioning in DFDs?
Answer: Data partitioning involves dividing a large system into smaller, more manageable sub-systems or processes, each with its own DFD.

4.5.27 Question: How do you document a DFD?
Answer: Document a DFD by providing descriptions for processes, data stores, data flows, and external entities, often supported by a data dictionary.

4.5.28 Question: What is the significance of data flow arrows in a DFD?
Answer: Data flow arrows indicate the direction of data movement between processes, data stores, and external entities, showing how data travels through the system.

4.5.29 Question: How can DFDs identify system inefficiencies?
Answer: DFDs can highlight bottlenecks, redundant processes, and unnecessary data flows, helping to identify and address system inefficiencies.

4.5.30 Question: What is the role of feedback loops in DFDs?
Answer: Feedback loops in DFDs represent data that is returned to an earlier process for validation or further processing, ensuring accuracy and completeness.

4.5.31 Question: How are control flows represented in DFDs?
Answer: Control flows are typically not represented in DFDs, as DFDs focus on the flow of data rather than control or decision-making processes.

4.5.32 Question: How can DFDs assist in system integration?
Answer: DFDs assist in system integration by clearly mapping data flows between different subsystems, ensuring seamless data exchange and integration.

4.5.33 Question: What is the difference between an internal and external entity in a DFD?
Answer: Internal entities are processes within the system, while external entities are outside the system's boundary but interact with it.

4.5.34 Question: Can a process have multiple inputs and outputs in a DFD?
Answer: Yes, a process can have multiple inputs and outputs, representing various data flows that are transformed within the process.

4.5.35 Question: How do you ensure consistency between different levels of DFDs?
Answer: Ensure consistency by maintaining the same data flow inputs and outputs when breaking down processes from higher to lower-level DFDs, and regularly reviewing them for accuracy.

4.6 Process Modelling Concepts

4.6.1 Question: What is process modelling in system analysis and design?
Answer: Process modelling is the technique of representing processes of a system, typically through graphical means, to analyse and improve the flow of information and tasks.

4.6.2 Question: Why is process modelling important?
Answer: Process modelling is important because it helps in understanding, analysing , and documenting the processes within a system, leading to improved efficiency and effectiveness.

4.6.3 Question: What is a data flow diagram (DFD)?
Answer: A DFD is a graphical representation of the flow of data through a system, showing data inputs, outputs, storage points, and pathways.

4.6.4 Question: What are the main components of a DFD?
Answer: The main components of a DFD are processes, data stores, data flows, and external entities.

4.6.5 Question: What is a context diagram?
Answer: A context diagram is a high-level DFD that shows the system's boundaries, external entities that interact with the system, and major data flows between them.

4.6.6 Question: How do level 0 and level 1 DFDs differ?
Answer: Level 0 DFDs, or context diagrams, show the system's major processes and data flows. Level 1 DFDs decompose these processes into more detailed sub-processes.

4.6.7 Question: What is process decomposition?
Answer: Process decomposition involves breaking down complex processes into simpler, more manageable sub-processes for detailed analysis and understanding.

4.6.8 Question: What is a flowchart?
Answer: A flowchart is a diagram that depicts the steps in a process using symbols like arrows, rectangles, and diamonds to illustrate decision points and process flows.

4.6.9 Question: What is a swimlane diagram?
Answer: A swimlane diagram is a type of flowchart that organizes activities into lanes representing different actors or departments, clarifying roles and responsibilities.

4.6.10 Question: What is business process modelling notation (BPMN)?
Answer: BPMN is a standard for business process modelling that provides a graphical notation for specifying business processes in a Business Process Diagram.

4.6.11 Question: What are the advantages of using BPMN?
Answer: BPMN advantages include providing a standardized method to model processes, enhancing communication among stakeholders, and supporting process analysis and improvement.

4.6.12 Question: What is an activity diagram?
Answer: An activity diagram is a UML diagram that models the workflow of a system, showing activities, decision points, and parallel processes.

4.6.13 Question: What is process reengineering?

Answer: Process reengineering involves redesigning business processes from the ground up to achieve significant improvements in performance, efficiency, and quality.

4.6.14 Question: How does process modelling help in system development?
Answer: Process modelling helps in identifying inefficiencies, understanding requirements, and designing systems that improve process performance and meet user needs.

4.6.15 Question: What is a use case in process modelling?
Answer: A use case describes how a user interacts with a system to achieve a specific goal, illustrating functional requirements and process flows.

4.6.16 Question: What is an event-driven process chain (EPC)?
Answer: EPC is a type of flowchart used for business process modelling that depicts the sequence of events and functions in a process.

4.6.17 Question: What is the purpose of a process map?
Answer: A process map visually represents the sequence of actions and decisions in a process, helping to analyse and improve process efficiency.

4.6.18 Question: What is the difference between a DFD and a flowchart?
Answer: A DFD focuses on the flow of data within a system, while a flowchart represents the sequence of steps in a process.

4.6.19 Question: What is process optimization?
Answer: Process optimization involves analysing and improving processes to maximize efficiency, reduce costs, and enhance performance.

4.6.20 Question: How do you validate a process model?
Answer: Validating a process model involves ensuring it accurately represents the real-world process, meets requirements, and effectively communicates information to stakeholders.

4.6.21 Question: What are the benefits of process modelling tools?
Answer: Process modelling tools provide visual representations, support collaboration, facilitate analysis, and improve documentation and communication of processes.

4.6.22 Question: What is workflow automation?
Answer: Workflow automation involves using technology to automate repeatable business processes, reducing manual effort and improving efficiency.

4.6.23 Question: What is the role of feedback in process modelling?
Answer: Feedback helps in refining and improving process models by incorporating insights and experiences from stakeholders and real-world operations.

4.6.24 Question: What is a process repository?
Answer: A process repository is a centralized database where process models, documentation, and related information are stored and managed.

4.6.25 Question: What is a Gantt chart in process modelling?
Answer: A Gantt chart is a visual project management tool that displays the schedule of tasks or activities, showing their durations and dependencies.

4.6.26 Question: What is the significance of bottlenecks in process modelling?
Answer: Identifying bottlenecks in a process helps in pinpointing areas of inefficiency and implementing changes to improve process flow and performance.

4.6.27 Question: What is a decision table?
Answer: A decision table is a tabular method for representing complex decision logic, outlining different conditions and corresponding actions.

4.6.28 Question: How does simulation support process modelling?
Answer: Simulation allows testing and analysing process models in a virtual environment, predicting performance and identifying potential issues before implementation.

4.6.29 Question: What is Six Sigma in process improvement?
Answer: Six Sigma is a data-driven methodology for improving process quality by identifying and eliminating defects and reducing variability.

4.6.30 Question: What is lean process modelling?
Answer: Lean process modelling focuses on creating value by eliminating waste and improving process efficiency and flow.

4.6.31 Question: What is the role of KPIs in process modelling?
Answer: Key Performance Indicators (KPIs) measure the effectiveness and efficiency of processes, guiding improvements and ensuring alignment with business goals.

4.6.32 Question: What is a SIPOC diagram?
Answer: A SIPOC diagram is a high-level process map that outlines Suppliers, Inputs, Processes, Outputs, and Customers, providing a comprehensive overview of a process.

4.6.33 Question: What is continuous improvement in process modelling?
Answer: Continuous improvement involves regularly analysing and refining processes to achieve incremental enhancements in performance and efficiency.

4.6.34 Question: What is a value stream map?
Answer: A value stream map visualizes the flow of materials and information through a process, highlighting value-adding and non-value-adding activities.

4.6.35 Question: How do you document a process model?
Answer: Documenting a process model involves creating detailed descriptions, diagrams, and supporting information to ensure clarity and facilitate communication and implementation.

4.7 Business Process Modelling Notation (BPMN)

4.7.1 Question: What is Business Process Modelling Notation (BPMN)?
Answer: BPMN is a graphical representation for specifying business processes in a business process model, providing a standard notation that is easily understandable by all business stakeholders.

4.7.2 Question: What are the key elements of BPMN?
Answer: Key elements of BPMN include flow objects (events, activities, gateways), connecting objects (sequence flow, message flow, association), Swimlanes, and artifacts.

4.7.3 Question: What is an event in BPMN?
Answer: An event is something that happens during the course of a business process, represented by a circle, and can be start, intermediate, or end events.

4.7.4 Question: What is an activity in BPMN?
Answer: An activity is a task or work that is performed within a business process, represented by a rounded rectangle.

4.7.5 Question: What is a gateway in BPMN?

Answer: A gateway is used to control the divergence and convergence of sequence flow, represented by a diamond shape, and can include types like exclusive, inclusive, and parallel gateways.

4.7.6 Question: What is a sequence flow in BPMN?
Answer: A sequence flow is used to show the order in which activities are performed in a process, represented by a solid arrow.

4.7.7 Question: What is a message flow in BPMN?
Answer: A message flow shows the flow of messages between two participants that are prepared to send and receive them, represented by a dashed arrow.

4.7.8 Question: What are Swimlanes in BPMN?
Answer: Swimlanes are used to organize and categorize activities in a process based on the roles or departments responsible for those activities, represented by pools and lanes.

4.7.9 Question: What is a pool in BPMN?
Answer: A pool represents a participant in a process, often used to represent an entire organization or an external entity.

4.7.10 Question: What is a lane in BPMN?
Answer: A lane is a sub-partition within a pool, used to organize and categorize activities within a pool based on roles, departments, or functions.

4.7.11 Question: What are artifacts in BPMN?
Answer: Artifacts provide additional information about the process and include data objects, groups, and annotations.

4.7.12 Question: What is a data object in BPMN?
Answer: A data object represents information flowing through the process, such as documents, emails, or databases.

4.7.13 Question: What is an annotation in BPMN?
Answer: An annotation provides additional textual information about a process element, represented by a bracketed text box.

4.7.14 Question: What is the purpose of BPMN?
Answer: The purpose of BPMN is to provide a standard way to model business processes, making them easier to understand and communicate among stakeholders.

4.7.15 Question: How does BPMN support process improvement?
Answer: BPMN supports process improvement by visually representing business processes, making it easier to identify inefficiencies and areas for enhancement.

4.7.16 Question: What is a sub-process in BPMN?
Answer: A sub-process is a compound activity that contains other activities, providing a way to encapsulate and simplify complex processes.

4.7.17 Question: What is a reusable sub-process in BPMN?
Answer: A reusable sub-process is a sub-process that can be called and executed from different parts of the process or from different processes.

4.7.18 Question: What is an event sub-process in BPMN?
Answer: An event sub-process is a special sub-process triggered by an event, providing a way to handle exceptions or interruptions in the process flow.

4.7.19 Question: What is a loop activity in BPMN?

Answer: A loop activity is an activity that repeats until a certain condition is met, represented by a small loop symbol at the bottom of the activity.

4.7.20 Question: What is a multi-instance activity in BPMN?
Answer: A multi-instance activity is an activity that occurs multiple times either sequentially or in parallel, indicated by three vertical lines at the bottom of the activity.

4.7.21 Question: What is a conditional event in BPMN?
Answer: A conditional event is triggered based on the evaluation of a condition, represented by a diamond inside a circle.

4.7.22 Question: What is a timer event in BPMN?
Answer: A timer event is triggered based on a specific time or date, represented by a clock inside a circle.

4.7.23 Question: What is an error event in BPMN?
Answer: An error event is used to handle errors within a process, typically resulting in an alternative flow, represented by a lightning bolt inside a circle.

4.7.24 Question: What is an escalation event in BPMN?
Answer: An escalation event indicates that a condition requiring urgent attention has occurred, allowing the process to take appropriate action, represented by a black arrow inside a circle.

4.7.25 Question: What is a boundary event in BPMN?
Answer: A boundary event is attached to the boundary of an activity and triggers an alternative flow when the event occurs, used for exception handling.

4.7.26 Question: What is a parallel gateway in BPMN?
Answer: A parallel gateway is used to split or merge multiple parallel paths in a process, allowing activities to occur simultaneously.

4.7.27 Question: What is an exclusive gateway in BPMN?
Answer: An exclusive gateway is used to create alternative paths in a process flow, where only one path can be taken based on a condition.

4.7.28 Question: What is an inclusive gateway in BPMN?
Answer: An inclusive gateway allows one or more paths to be taken, depending on the conditions specified for each path.

4.7.29 Question: What is a complex gateway in BPMN?
Answer: A complex gateway is used for complex synchronization behaviour, allowing multiple paths to be taken based on specific rules.

4.7.30 Question: What is a message event in BPMN?
Answer: A message event indicates that a message has been sent or received, used to represent communication between different participants.

4.8 Process Improvement Techniques

4.8.1 Question: What is process improvement?
Answer: Process improvement involves identifying, analysing, and enhancing existing business processes to optimize performance, increase efficiency, and reduce waste.

4.8.2 Question: Why is process improvement important in system analysis and design?
Answer: Process improvement ensures that systems operate more efficiently, effectively meet business needs, and provide better quality outcomes.

4.8.3 Question: What is the PDCA cycle?

Answer: The PDCA cycle, also known as Plan-Do-Check-Act, is a four-step model for carrying out process improvement and ensuring continuous improvement.

4.8.4 Question: What is Six Sigma?

Answer: Six Sigma is a data-driven methodology aimed at reducing defects and variability in processes to improve quality and efficiency.

4.8.5 Question: What are the key principles of Lean methodology?

Answer: Lean methodology focuses on minimizing waste, improving process flow, and delivering value to the customer by optimizing resources and processes.

4.8.6 Question: What is value stream mapping?

Answer: Value stream mapping is a Lean tool that visually maps out all steps in a process, helping to identify waste and areas for improvement.

4.8.7 Question: What is the purpose of root cause analysis?

Answer: Root cause analysis identifies the underlying causes of problems or defects to prevent recurrence and ensure long-term solutions.

4.8.8 Question: What is Kaizen?

Answer: Kaizen is a Japanese term meaning "continuous improvement," emphasizing small, incremental changes to improve processes and efficiency.

4.8.9 Question: How does benchmarking support process improvement?

Answer: Benchmarking involves comparing processes, performance metrics, and best practices against industry standards to identify improvement opportunities.

4.8.10 Question: What is a fishbone diagram?

Answer: A fishbone diagram, or Ishikawa diagram, is a visual tool used to identify and analyse the root causes of problems in a process.

4.8.11 Question: What is Business Process Reengineering (BPR)?

Answer: BPR is a radical approach to process improvement that involves redesigning business processes from the ground up to achieve dramatic improvements in performance.

4.8.12 Question: What role does automation play in process improvement?

Answer: Automation streamlines processes by reducing manual tasks, minimizing errors, and increasing efficiency and consistency.

4.8.13 Question: What is Total Quality Management (TQM)?

Answer: TQM is a management approach focused on continuous improvement, customer satisfaction, and the involvement of all employees in quality initiatives.

4.8.14 Question: How can process mapping help in process improvement?

Answer: Process mapping visually represents workflows, helping to identify inefficiencies, bottlenecks, and areas for improvement.

4.8.15 Question: What is the significance of performance metrics in process improvement?

Answer: Performance metrics provide quantitative data to measure process efficiency, effectiveness, and the impact of improvement initiatives.

4.8.16 Question: What is the role of a process improvement team?

Answer: A process improvement team collaborates to analyse processes, identify issues, propose solutions, and implement improvements.

4.8.17 Question: What is DMAIC in Six Sigma?
Answer: DMAIC stands for Define, Measure, Analyse, Improve, Control—a structured problem-solving process used in Six Sigma projects.

4.8.18 Question: How does change management relate to process improvement?
Answer: Change management ensures that process improvements are implemented smoothly and sustainably by managing the transition and addressing resistance.

4.8.19 Question: What is continuous improvement?
Answer: Continuous improvement is an ongoing effort to enhance processes, products, or services through incremental and breakthrough improvements.

4.8.20 Question: What is a bottleneck in a process?
Answer: A bottleneck is a point in a process where the flow is restricted, causing delays and reducing overall efficiency.

4.8.21 Question: What is the role of feedback in process improvement?
Answer: Feedback provides insights into process performance, helping to identify areas for improvement and measure the impact of changes.

4.8.22 Question: What is process standardization?
Answer: Process standardization involves establishing uniform procedures and practices to ensure consistency and efficiency across the organization.

4.8.23 Question: What is the significance of process documentation?
Answer: Process documentation records procedures, guidelines, and workflows, providing a reference for training, compliance, and continuous improvement.

4.8.24 Question: How does customer feedback contribute to process improvement?
Answer: Customer feedback highlights areas where processes may not meet expectations, guiding improvements to enhance satisfaction and quality.

4.8.25 Question: What is the role of technology in process improvement?
Answer: Technology enhances process improvement by enabling automation, data analysis, and real-time monitoring, leading to more efficient and effective operations.

4.8.26 Question: What is a control chart?
Answer: A control chart is a statistical tool used to monitor process variability and stability over time, identifying trends and deviations from standards.

4.8.27 Question: What is the importance of training in process improvement?
Answer: Training ensures that employees have the necessary skills and knowledge to implement and sustain process improvements effectively.

4.8.28 Question: What is a process audit?
Answer: A process audit reviews and evaluates the effectiveness, efficiency, and compliance of processes, identifying opportunities for improvement.

4.8.29 Question: What is the 5S methodology?
Answer: The 5S methodology focuses on workplace organization and efficiency through five steps: Sort, Set in order, Shine, Standardize, and Sustain.

4.8.30 Question: How does project management integrate with process improvement?
Answer: Project management provides structured approaches and tools to plan, execute, and monitor process improvement initiatives, ensuring successful outcomes.

Online Resources

More Practices Questions

Online Exam Paper
URL
https://forms.gle/KgsXR2t179nKxqDaA
QR Code

YouTube Video Playlist Link

Chapter 4
URL
https://www.youtube.com/playlist?list=PLzlh_31VWEFp1avLnfoicm5UN230oUD_y
QR Code

Chapter 5: Database Fundamentals

5.1 Database Fundamentals

5.1.1 Question: What is a database?
Answer: A database is an organized collection of data that is stored and accessed electronically, designed to efficiently manage, retrieve, and update data.

5.1.2 Question: What is a DBMS (Database Management System)?
Answer: A DBMS is software that provides tools to create, manage, and manipulate databases, ensuring data integrity, security, and efficient access.

5.1.3 Question: What are the different types of databases?
Answer: The main types of databases are relational databases, NoSQL databases, object-oriented databases, and distributed databases.

5.1.4 Question: Can you explain the concept of a relational database?
Answer: A relational database organizes data into tables (relations) with rows and columns, using SQL for data manipulation and enforcing relationships through keys.

5.1.5 Question: What is SQL?
Answer: SQL (Structured Query Language) is a standard programming language used to manage and manipulate relational databases.

5.1.6 Question: What are primary keys and foreign keys?
Answer: A primary key uniquely identifies each record in a table, while a foreign key establishes a relationship between two tables by referencing the primary key in another table.

5.1.7 Question: What is normalization in database design?
Answer: Normalization is the process of organizing data to reduce redundancy and improve data integrity by dividing larger tables into smaller, related tables.

5.1.8 Question: What are the normal forms in normalization?
Answer: Normal forms include 1NF, 2NF, 3NF, BCNF, and higher forms, each addressing specific types of redundancy and dependency in tables.

5.1.9 Question: What is denormalization?
Answer: Denormalization is the process of combining normalized tables to improve read performance, often at the cost of increased redundancy.

5.1.10 Question: What is an index in a database?
Answer: An index is a data structure that improves the speed of data retrieval operations on a table by providing quick access to rows.

5.1.11 Question: What are the types of indexes?
Answer: Types of indexes include primary indexes, secondary indexes, unique indexes, and composite indexes.

5.1.12 Question: What is a transaction in database terms?
Answer: A transaction is a sequence of operations performed as a single logical unit of work, ensuring data consistency and integrity.

5.1.13 Question: What are ACID properties?
Answer: ACID properties (Atomicity, Consistency, Isolation, Durability) ensure reliable processing of database transactions.

5.1.14 Question: What is a join operation in SQL?
Answer: A join operation combines rows from two or more tables based on a related column, enabling complex queries across multiple tables.

5.1.15 Question: What are the types of joins in SQL?
Answer: Types of joins include inner join, left join, right join, and full outer join, each specifying how tables are combined.

5.1.16 Question: What is a view in a database?
Answer: A view is a virtual table based on the result set of a query, providing a way to simplify complex queries and enhance security by limiting data access.

5.1.17 Question: What is a stored procedure?
Answer: A stored procedure is a precompiled collection of SQL statements stored in the database, used to encapsulate business logic and improve performance.

5.1.18 Question: What is a trigger in a database?
Answer: A trigger is a set of SQL statements that automatically execute in response to certain events on a table, such as insertions, updates, or deletions.

5.1.19 Question: What is a schema in a database?
Answer: A schema is the logical structure that defines how data is organized in a database, including tables, views, indexes, and relationships.

5.1.20 Question: What is data integrity?
Answer: Data integrity refers to the accuracy, consistency, and reliability of data stored in a database, maintained through constraints, rules, and ACID properties.

5.1.21 Question: What is a NoSQL database?
Answer: NoSQL databases are non-relational databases designed for flexible data models, horizontal scaling, and high performance, often used for big data and real-time applications.

5.1.22 Question: What are the types of NoSQL databases?
Answer: Types of NoSQL databases include document databases, key-value stores, column-family stores, and graph databases.

5.1.23 Question: What is a data warehouse?
Answer: A data warehouse is a centralized repository designed for storing, managing, and analysing large volumes of structured and semi-structured data from multiple sources.

5.1.24 Question: What is ETL in the context of data warehousing?
Answer: ETL (Extract, Transform, Load) is the process of extracting data from various sources, transforming it into a suitable format, and loading it into a data warehouse.

5.1.25 Question: What is data mining?
Answer: Data mining is the process of discovering patterns, correlations, and insights from large datasets using statistical and computational techniques.

5.1.26 Question: What is a distributed database?
Answer: A distributed database is a database where data is stored across multiple physical locations, connected by a network, providing redundancy and high availability.

5.1.27 Question: What is database replication?
Answer: Database replication is the process of copying data from one database to another to ensure consistency and improve availability and reliability.

5.1.28 Question: What is sharding in databases?
Answer: Sharding is a database partitioning technique that divides a large dataset into smaller, more manageable pieces called shards, which are distributed across multiple servers.

5.1.29 Question: What is a graph database?
Answer: A graph database uses graph structures with nodes, edges, and properties to represent and store data, excelling at managing relationships and interconnected data.

5.1.30 Question: What is a cloud database?
Answer: A cloud database is a database service built and accessed through a cloud platform, offering scalability, flexibility, and reduced infrastructure management.

5.1.31 Question: What is database security?
Answer: Database security involves measures and practices to protect the database from unauthorized access, threats, and vulnerabilities, ensuring data confidentiality, integrity, and availability.

5.1.32 Question: What is SQL injection?
Answer: SQL injection is a type of attack that exploits vulnerabilities in a database application by injecting malicious SQL code to manipulate or access unauthorized data.

5.1.33 Question: What is data backup?
Answer: Data backup is the process of creating copies of data to protect against data loss or corruption, ensuring data can be restored in case of a failure.

5.1.34 Question: What is a relational algebra in databases?
Answer: Relational algebra is a formal language for relational databases that provides a set of operations to manipulate and query data, forming the theoretical foundation for SQL.

5.1.35 Question: What is a data dictionary?
Answer: A data dictionary is a centralized repository of metadata that contains definitions, relationships, and attributes of data elements in a database, aiding in data management and governance.

5.2 Entity-Relationship Modelling

5.2.1 Question: What is an Entity-Relationship Model (ERM)?
Answer: An ERM is a data modelling technique that visually represents the structure of a database, showing entities, their attributes, and the relationships between them.

5.2.2 Question: What is an entity in ER modelling?
Answer: An entity is a real-world object or concept that can be distinctly identified and stored in a database, such as a customer, product, or order.

5.2.3 Question: What are attributes in an ER model?
Answer: Attributes are properties or characteristics of an entity, such as a customer's name, address, or phone number.

5.2.4 Question: What is a primary key in an ER model?
Answer: A primary key is a unique identifier for an entity, ensuring that each record in the database can be uniquely identified.

5.2.5 Question: What is a relationship in ER modelling?
Answer: A relationship defines how entities interact with each other, representing associations like "orders placed by customers" or "students enrolled in courses."

5.2.6 Question: What are the types of relationships in ER modelling?

Answer: The main types of relationships are one-to-one, one-to-many, and many-to-many.

5.2.7 Question: What is a one-to-one relationship?
Answer: A one-to-one relationship exists when a single instance of an entity is associated with a single instance of another entity.

5.2.8 Question: What is a one-to-many relationship?
Answer: A one-to-many relationship occurs when a single instance of an entity is associated with multiple instances of another entity.

5.2.9 Question: What is a many-to-many relationship?
Answer: A many-to-many relationship exists when multiple instances of an entity are associated with multiple instances of another entity.

5.2.10 Question: What is a composite key?
Answer: A composite key is a combination of two or more attributes that uniquely identify an entity in the database.

5.2.11 Question: What is a foreign key?
Answer: A foreign key is an attribute in one table that links to the primary key of another table, establishing a relationship between the two tables.

5.2.12 Question: What is an ER diagram (ERD)?
Answer: An ERD is a graphical representation of the ER model, depicting entities, attributes, and relationships.

5.2.13 Question: What is cardinality in ER modelling?
Answer: Cardinality specifies the number of instances of one entity that can be associated with instances of another entity.

5.2.14 Question: What is participation in ER modelling?
Answer: Participation indicates whether all or only some entity instances participate in a relationship, categorized as total or partial participation.

5.2.15 Question: What is a weak entity?
Answer: A weak entity is an entity that cannot be uniquely identified by its own attributes alone and relies on a foreign key from another entity.

5.2.16 Question: What is a strong entity?
Answer: A strong entity can be uniquely identified by its own attributes without relying on a foreign key from another entity.

5.2.17 Question: What is generalization in ER modelling?
Answer: Generalization is the process of abstracting common characteristics from multiple entities into a single, generalized entity.

5.2.18 Question: What is specialization in ER modelling?
Answer: Specialization is the process of creating new, specialized entities from an existing entity based on certain attributes or relationships.

5.2.19 Question: What is aggregation in ER modelling?
Answer: Aggregation is a higher-level abstraction that treats relationships as higher-level entities, useful for representing complex relationships.

5.2.20 Question: What is normalization in the context of ER modelling?
Answer: Normalization is the process of organizing data to reduce redundancy and improve data integrity by dividing larger tables into smaller, related tables.

5.2.21 Question: What is the purpose of an ER model?
Answer: The ER model helps in designing a database structure that is logically consistent and aligned with the business requirements, ensuring efficient data management.

5.2.22 Question: What is the difference between ER model and relational model?
Answer: The ER model is a high-level conceptual design, while the relational model is the implementation of that design in a relational database system.

5.2.23 Question: How are relationships represented in an ER diagram?
Answer: Relationships in an ER diagram are represented by diamond shapes connecting the entities, often annotated with cardinality and participation constraints.

5.2.24 Question: What are multi-valued attributes?
Answer: Multi-valued attributes are attributes that can have multiple values for a single entity instance, such as a person's multiple phone numbers.

5.2.25 Question: What are derived attributes?
Answer: Derived attributes are attributes whose values can be calculated or derived from other attributes in the database, such as age calculated from birth date.

5.2.26 Question: What is a ternary relationship?
Answer: A ternary relationship is a relationship involving three entities, indicating how they interact simultaneously.

5.2.27 Question: What is a recursive relationship?
Answer: A recursive relationship is a relationship between instances of the same entity, such as an employee supervising other employees.

5.2.28 Question: How do you handle many-to-many relationships in a relational database?
Answer: Many-to-many relationships are typically handled by creating an associative or junction table that includes foreign keys from both related entities.

5.2.29 Question: What is a surrogate key?
Answer: A surrogate key is a system-generated unique identifier for an entity, often used when a natural primary key is not available or practical.

5.2.30 Question: What is an identifying relationship?
Answer: An identifying relationship is a relationship where the child entity's primary key includes the primary key of the parent entity, indicating dependence.

5.2.31 Question: What is a non-identifying relationship?
Answer: A non-identifying relationship is a relationship where the child entity's primary key does not include the primary key of the parent entity, indicating independence.

5.2.32 Question: What is the difference between entity and table?
Answer: An entity is a conceptual representation of a real-world object, while a table is a physical implementation of an entity in a relational database.

5.2.33 Question: What is the difference between an attribute and a field?
Answer: An attribute is a property of an entity, while a field is a column in a table representing that attribute in a database.

5.2.34 Question: What is the role of ER modelling in database design?
Answer: ER modelling plays a crucial role in database design by providing a clear and structured way to define and visualize the data requirements and relationships.

5.2.35 Question: How does ER modelling improve data integrity?

Answer: ER modelling improves data integrity by clearly defining relationships and constraints, ensuring data is consistent, accurate, and aligned with business rules.

5.3 Normalization

5.3.1 Question: What is normalization in database design?

Answer: Normalization is the process of organizing data in a database to reduce redundancy and improve data integrity by dividing large tables into smaller, related tables.

5.3.2 Question: What is the main goal of normalization?

Answer: The main goal of normalization is to eliminate redundant data and ensure data dependencies make sense to reduce anomalies during data operations.

5.3.3 Question: What is a functional dependency in the context of normalization?

Answer: A functional dependency occurs when one attribute uniquely determines another attribute in a database table, crucial for defining normal forms.

5.3.4 Question: What is the First Normal Form (1NF)?

Answer: The First Normal Form (1NF) ensures that the values in each column of a table are atomic and each column contains only one value for each row.

5.3.5 Question: What is the Second Normal Form (2NF)?

Answer: The Second Normal Form (2NF) builds on 1NF by ensuring that all non-key attributes are fully functionally dependent on the primary key, eliminating partial dependencies.

5.3.6 Question: What is the Third Normal Form (3NF)?

Answer: The Third Normal Form (3NF) ensures that all attributes are functionally dependent only on the primary key, eliminating transitive dependencies.

5.3.7 Question: What is the Boyce-Codd Normal Form (BCNF)?

Answer: BCNF is an extension of 3NF that ensures every determinant is a candidate key, addressing certain types of anomalies not covered by 3NF.

5.3.8 Question: What is the Fourth Normal Form (4NF)?

Answer: The Fourth Normal Form (4NF) deals with multi-valued dependencies, ensuring that there are no non-trivial multi-valued dependencies in a table.

5.3.9 Question: What is the Fifth Normal Form (5NF)?

Answer: The Fifth Normal Form (5NF) addresses join dependencies, ensuring that data is decomposed into smaller tables without losing information or introducing redundancy.

5.3.10 Question: What are the benefits of normalization?

Answer: Benefits of normalization include reduced data redundancy, improved data integrity, easier maintenance, and efficient data retrieval.

5.3.11 Question: What are the potential drawbacks of normalization?

Answer: Potential drawbacks include increased complexity of database design, potential performance issues due to multiple table joins, and the need for thorough understanding of dependencies.

5.3.12 Question: What is denormalization?

Answer: Denormalization is the process of combining tables to reduce the number of joins and improve read performance, often used when query performance is more critical than data redundancy.

5.3.13 Question: Can you explain a scenario where denormalization might be beneficial?

Answer: Denormalization can be beneficial in a data warehousing scenario where complex queries need to be executed quickly and data redundancy is acceptable.

5.3.14 Question: What is a primary key?
Answer: A primary key is a unique identifier for a record in a database table, ensuring that each record can be uniquely identified.

5.3.15 Question: What is a candidate key?
Answer: A candidate key is an attribute or a set of attributes that can uniquely identify a record in a table and can be chosen as the primary key.

5.3.16 Question: What is a composite key?
Answer: A composite key is a primary key composed of two or more attributes, used to uniquely identify a record in a table when a single attribute is not sufficient.

5.3.17 Question: What is a foreign key?
Answer: A foreign key is an attribute in one table that links to the primary key of another table, establishing a relationship between the two tables.

5.3.18 Question: What is an anomaly in database design?
Answer: Anomalies are problems such as update, insert, and delete anomalies that arise due to redundancy and poor database design, which normalization aims to eliminate.

5.3.19 Question: What is an update anomaly?
Answer: An update anomaly occurs when changes to data in a database are not consistently applied, leading to data inconsistency.

5.3.20 Question: What is an insert anomaly?
Answer: An insert anomaly occurs when certain data cannot be inserted into the database without the presence of other data, often due to improper database design.

5.3.21 Question: What is a delete anomaly?
Answer: A delete anomaly occurs when deleting data unintentionally removes additional, needed information due to database design flaws.

5.3.22 Question: What is a transitive dependency?
Answer: A transitive dependency exists when a non-key attribute depends on another non-key attribute, which 3NF aims to eliminate.

5.3.23 Question: What is a multi-valued dependency?
Answer: A multi-valued dependency occurs when one attribute in a table uniquely determines another attribute independently of other attributes, addressed by 4NF.

5.3.24 Question: How does normalization improve data integrity?
Answer: Normalization improves data integrity by organizing data to reduce redundancy, ensuring consistency, and enforcing relationships through constraints.

5.3.25 Question: What is data redundancy?
Answer: Data redundancy occurs when the same piece of data is stored in multiple places within a database, leading to wasted storage and potential inconsistencies.

5.3.26 Question: What is data integrity?
Answer: Data integrity refers to the accuracy and consistency of data over its lifecycle, ensured through constraints, normalization, and validation rules.

5.3.27 Question: What is a surrogate key?

Answer: A surrogate key is an artificial key created for a table, typically an auto-incrementing number, used as a primary key instead of a natural key.

5.3.28 Question: How does normalization affect database performance?
Answer: While normalization reduces redundancy and improves data integrity, it can sometimes lead to performance issues due to the need for multiple table joins in complex queries.

5.3.29 Question: What is a dependency diagram?
Answer: A dependency diagram visually represents the dependencies between attributes in a database table, used to identify and eliminate anomalies through normalization.

5.3.30 Question: What is referential integrity?
Answer: Referential integrity ensures that foreign key values in a table correctly correspond to primary key values in another table, maintaining consistency across related tables.

5.3.31 Question: What is a natural key?
Answer: A natural key is an attribute that naturally identifies a record, such as a social security number or email address, as opposed to a surrogate key.

5.3.32 Question: What is an index in a database?
Answer: An index is a database structure that improves the speed of data retrieval operations by providing quick access to rows in a table based on the values of one or more columns.

5.3.33 Question: How does normalization support scalability?
Answer: Normalization supports scalability by organizing data efficiently, reducing redundancy, and ensuring that the database can grow and handle increased load without performance degradation.

5.3.34 Question: What is an ERD in the context of normalization?
Answer: An Entity-Relationship Diagram (ERD) is a graphical representation of entities and their relationships, used to design and normalize database structures.

5.3.35 Question: What is a relational schema?
Answer: A relational schema is the blueprint of a database that defines how data is organized into tables, including the tables' structure, relationships, and constraints.

Online Resources

More Practices Questions

Online Exam Paper
URL
https://forms.gle/fUUtrZQoSiUE2Q4D7

QR Code

YouTube Video Playlist Link

Chapter 5
URL
https://www.youtube.com/playlist?list=PLzlh_31VWEFpYufGWpiwqc2ZQAS0fsoHu
QR Code

Chapter 6: Advanced Database Design

6.1 Database Design

6.1.1 Question: What is database design?
Answer: Database design is the process of creating a detailed data model of a database, defining the structure, storage, and retrieval mechanisms to ensure data integrity and performance.

6.1.2 Question: What are the main objectives of database design?
Answer: The main objectives are to ensure data consistency, integrity, security, and efficient access, supporting the requirements of the application and its users.

6.1.3 Question: What is normalization in database design?
Answer: Normalization is the process of organizing data to reduce redundancy and improve data integrity by dividing a database into two or more tables and defining relationships between the tables.

6.1.4 Question: What are the normal forms in database normalization?
Answer: The normal forms include 1NF (First Normal Form), 2NF (Second Normal Form), 3NF (Third Normal Form), BCNF (Boyce-Codd Normal Form), and higher normal forms.

6.1.5 Question: What is denormalization and why is it used?
Answer: Denormalization is the process of combining normalized tables to improve read performance, used when queries require complex joins that degrade performance.

6.1.6 Question: Can you explain what a primary key is?
Answer: A primary key is a unique identifier for a record in a table, ensuring that each record can be uniquely identified.

6.1.7 Question: What is a foreign key in database design?
Answer: A foreign key is a field in one table that uniquely identifies a row in another table, establishing a relationship between the two tables.

6.1.8 Question: What is an index in a database?
Answer: An index is a database object that improves the speed of data retrieval operations on a table by providing quick access to rows.

6.1.9 Question: What are the types of indexes?
Answer: Types of indexes include primary indexes, secondary indexes, unique indexes, and non-unique indexes.

6.1.10 Question: What is a composite key?
Answer: A composite key is a combination of two or more columns in a table that together serve as a unique identifier for a row.

6.1.11 Question: What is referential integrity?
Answer: Referential integrity ensures that relationships between tables remain consistent, where foreign keys correctly and accurately reference primary keys.

6.1.12 Question: What is a database schema?
Answer: A database schema is the blueprint or architecture of a database, defining how data is organized and how relationships are established.

6.1.13 Question: What is an entity-relationship (ER) diagram?
Answer: An ER diagram is a graphical representation of entities and their relationships, used in database design to model the logical structure of a database.

6.1.14 Question: What is a surrogate key?
Answer: A surrogate key is an artificial key assigned to a table as a unique identifier, often a sequential number, unrelated to the actual data.

6.1.15 Question: What is data integrity in database design?
Answer: Data integrity refers to the accuracy and consistency of data over its lifecycle, maintained through constraints, keys, and rules.

6.1.16 Question: What is a relational database?
Answer: A relational database organizes data into tables with rows and columns, using relationships defined by keys to link data.

6.1.17 Question: What is a transaction in a database?
Answer: A transaction is a sequence of operations performed as a single logical unit of work, ensuring data consistency and integrity.

6.1.18 Question: What are ACID properties?
Answer: ACID properties (Atomicity, Consistency, Isolation, Durability) ensure reliable processing of database transactions.

6.1.19 Question: What is a database trigger?
Answer: A database trigger is a procedural code that is automatically executed in response to certain events on a particular table or view.

6.1.20 Question: What is a stored procedure?
Answer: A stored procedure is a precompiled collection of SQL statements and optional control-of-flow statements stored under a name and processed as a unit.

6.1.21 Question: What is a database view?
Answer: A database view is a virtual table representing the result of a SQL query, providing a way to simplify complex queries and enhance security.

6.1.22 Question: What is data modelling?
Answer: Data modelling is the process of creating a data model to represent data structures and relationships, typically using ER diagrams.

6.1.23 Question: What is a data warehouse?
Answer: A data warehouse is a centralized repository designed for query and analysis, storing large amounts of historical data.

6.1.24 Question: What is OLTP?
Answer: OLTP (Online Transaction Processing) systems manage transaction-oriented applications, emphasizing speed and efficiency for routine data operations.

6.1.25 Question: What is OLAP?
Answer: OLAP (Online Analytical Processing) systems support complex analysis and querying of large volumes of data, often used in data warehousing.

6.1.26 Question: What is database partitioning?
Answer: Database partitioning involves dividing a database into smaller, more manageable pieces, improving performance and manageability.

6.1.27 Question: What is database sharding?
Answer: Database sharding is a type of partitioning where data is horizontally partitioned across multiple databases or servers to distribute load.

6.1.28 Question: What is a NoSQL database?
Answer: NoSQL databases are non-relational databases designed for large-scale data storage and real-time web applications, offering flexibility and scalability.

6.1.29 Question: What is a graph database?
Answer: A graph database uses graph structures with nodes, edges, and properties to represent and store data, ideal for managing and querying complex relationships.

6.1.30 Question: What is data denormalization?
Answer: Data denormalization is the process of combining normalized tables to optimize read performance, often at the expense of write performance and data redundancy.

6.1.31 Question: What is a database constraint?
Answer: A database constraint enforces rules at the database level to ensure the integrity, accuracy, and reliability of the data.

6.1.32 Question: What is data redundancy?
Answer: Data redundancy occurs when the same piece of data is stored in multiple places, which can lead to data anomalies and increased storage costs.

6.1.33 Question: What is data consistency?
Answer: Data consistency ensures that data remains accurate and consistent across the database, particularly during transactions.

6.1.34 Question: What is the purpose of a unique key?
Answer: A unique key ensures that all values in a column or a combination of columns are unique across the table, preventing duplicate entries.

6.1.35 Question: What is database scalability?
Answer: Database scalability is the ability of a database to handle increased loads by adding resources such as hardware or optimizing the database design and queries.

6.2 Architectural Design

6.2.1 Question: What is software architecture?
Answer: Software architecture is the high-level structure of a software system, defining its components, their relationships, and the principles guiding its design and evolution.

6.2.2 Question: Why is architectural design important in software development?
Answer: Architectural design is crucial as it ensures the system is scalable, maintainable, and meets both functional and non-functional requirements.

6.2.3 Question: What are architectural patterns?
Answer: Architectural patterns are reusable solutions to common problems in software architecture, such as MVC (Model-View-Controller) and Microservices.

6.2.4 Question: Can you explain the Model-View-Controller (MVC) pattern?
Answer: MVC separates the application into three interconnected components: Model (data), View (UI), and Controller (business logic), promoting modularity and ease of maintenance.

6.2.5 Question: What is a Microservices architecture?
Answer: Microservices architecture breaks down an application into small, loosely coupled services, each running independently and communicating over a network.

6.2.6 Question: What are the benefits of Microservices architecture?

Answer: Benefits include improved scalability, independent deployment, fault isolation, and ease of integrating new technologies.

6.2.7 Question: What is a monolithic architecture?
Answer: A monolithic architecture is a single-tiered software application where all functions are managed and served from a single platform.

6.2.8 Question: What are the drawbacks of monolithic architecture?
Answer: Drawbacks include limited scalability, difficulty in managing large codebases, and challenges in deploying and maintaining the application.

6.2.9 Question: What is service-oriented architecture (SOA)?
Answer: SOA is a design pattern where services are provided to other components by application components, using a communication protocol over a network.

6.2.10 Question: What is a layered architecture?
Answer: Layered architecture divides the system into layers, each with specific responsibilities, promoting separation of concerns and ease of maintenance.

6.2.11 Question: What is the role of an architect in software development?
Answer: A software architect designs the overall structure of the system, makes high-level design choices, and ensures that the architecture aligns with business goals and requirements.

6.2.12 Question: What is the difference between software architecture and design?
Answer: Software architecture focuses on the high-level structure and overall framework of the system, while design deals with the implementation details and lower-level components.

6.2.13 Question: What is a reference architecture?
Answer: Reference architecture provides a template solution for an architecture for a particular domain, including a common vocabulary and set of conventions.

6.2.14 Question: What are the key qualities of a good software architecture?
Answer: Key qualities include scalability, maintainability, performance, security, and robustness.

6.2.15 Question: What is the purpose of architectural documentation?
Answer: Architectural documentation captures the architecture design decisions, rationale, and constraints, serving as a reference for developers and stakeholders.

6.2.16 Question: What is an API gateway in Microservices architecture?
Answer: An API gateway acts as a single entry point for all client interactions, routing requests to the appropriate microservices.

6.2.17 Question: What is the significance of scalability in architecture design?
Answer: Scalability ensures that the system can handle growth in workload and user demand without compromising performance.

6.2.18 Question: What is a distributed architecture?
Answer: Distributed architecture involves multiple interconnected components located on different networked computers, working together to achieve a common goal.

6.2.19 Question: What are the advantages of distributed architecture?
Answer: Advantages include improved fault tolerance, scalability, and resource sharing.

6.2.20 Question: What is fault tolerance in architectural design?
Answer: Fault tolerance is the ability of a system to continue functioning properly in the event of the failure of some of its components.

6.2.21 Question: What is an event-driven architecture?

Answer: Event-driven architecture is a design paradigm in which system components communicate and respond to events, enhancing decoupling and scalability.

6.2.22 Question: What is a container in software architecture?

Answer: A container is a lightweight, stand-alone, executable package that includes everything needed to run a piece of software, including code, runtime, system tools, and libraries.

6.2.23 Question: How do containers benefit software architecture?

Answer: Containers provide consistency across multiple development environments, improve resource efficiency, and enhance deployment scalability and portability.

6.2.24 Question: What is the importance of security in software architecture?

Answer: Security ensures that the system protects data and resources from unauthorized access, breaches, and other vulnerabilities.

6.2.25 Question: What is an architectural style?

Answer: An architectural style is a family of architectures that share certain characteristics, such as REST, which is used in designing networked applications.

6.2.26 Question: What is RESTful architecture?

Answer: RESTful architecture is based on representational state transfer principles, using stateless communication and standard HTTP methods for interaction.

6.2.27 Question: What is a serverless architecture?

Answer: Serverless architecture allows developers to build and run applications without managing server infrastructure, with services managed by cloud providers.

6.2.28 Question: What are the benefits of serverless architecture?

Answer: Benefits include reduced operational complexity, automatic scaling, and cost-efficiency based on actual usage.

6.2.29 Question: What is the significance of performance optimization in architectural design?

Answer: Performance optimization ensures the system meets required performance metrics, such as response time and throughput, enhancing user experience.

6.2.30 Question: What is a message queue in software architecture?

Answer: A message queue is a component that facilitates asynchronous communication between system components, improving system resilience and scalability.

6.3 Interface Design

6.3.1 Question: What is interface design in system analysis?

Answer: Interface design is the process of creating a user interface that facilitates interaction between the user and the system, focusing on usability and user experience.

6.3.2 Question: Why is interface design important in system development?

Answer: Interface design is crucial because it directly affects user satisfaction and productivity, making the system intuitive and easy to use.

6.3.3 Question: What are the key principles of good interface design?

Answer: Key principles include simplicity, consistency, visibility, feedback, tolerance, and affordance, ensuring a user-friendly experience.

6.3.4 Question: What is user-centred design?

Answer: User-centred design is an approach that focuses on the needs, preferences, and limitations of the end users at every stage of the design process.

6.3.5 Question: What are wireframes in interface design?
Answer: Wireframes are basic, low-fidelity visual representations of a user interface, used to outline the structure and layout of a design.

6.3.6 Question: What is the role of prototypes in interface design?
Answer: Prototypes are interactive, high-fidelity representations of a user interface used for testing and refining design concepts before full development.

6.3.7 Question: What is usability testing?
Answer: Usability testing involves evaluating a system's interface by observing real users as they interact with it to identify usability issues and areas for improvement.

6.3.8 Question: Can you explain the concept of responsive design?
Answer: Responsive design ensures that a user interface adapts smoothly to different screen sizes and devices, providing an optimal user experience on any platform.

6.3.9 Question: What are personas in interface design?
Answer: Personas are fictional characters created based on user research to represent different user types that might use the system, guiding design decisions.

6.3.10 Question: What is a user journey?
Answer: A user journey maps out the steps a user takes to complete a task within the system, highlighting pain points and opportunities for improvement.

6.3.11 Question: What is the significance of accessibility in interface design?
Answer: Accessibility ensures that a system is usable by people with various disabilities, complying with standards and enhancing inclusivity.

6.3.12 Question: What is heuristic evaluation?
Answer: Heuristic evaluation is a usability inspection method where experts use established heuristics to identify usability problems in a user interface.

6.3.13 Question: What are design patterns in interface design?
Answer: Design patterns are reusable solutions to common design problems, helping to create consistent and efficient user interfaces.

6.3.14 Question: What is information architecture?
Answer: Information architecture involves organizing and structuring information within a system to improve findability and usability.

6.3.15 Question: What is the role of feedback in interface design?
Answer: Feedback provides users with information about the result of their actions, enhancing their understanding and control of the system.

6.3.16 Question: What is the significance of consistency in interface design?
Answer: Consistency ensures that similar elements behave in predictable ways, reducing the learning curve and increasing user confidence.

6.3.17 Question: What is a style guide?
Answer: A style guide is a document that outlines design standards and guidelines, ensuring a consistent look and feel across the system.

6.3.18 Question: What is the importance of error messages in interface design?

Answer: Effective error messages help users understand what went wrong and how to fix it, reducing frustration and improving the overall user experience.

6.3.19 Question: What is a modal dialog?
Answer: A modal dialog is a pop-up window that requires the user to interact with it before returning to the main interface, used for critical interactions.

6.3.20 Question: What is a breadcrumb in web design?
Answer: Breadcrumbs are a navigation aid that shows users their current location within the system's hierarchy, helping them navigate more easily.

6.3.21 Question: What is the purpose of a dashboard in an interface?
Answer: A dashboard provides a visual summary of key information and metrics, allowing users to quickly assess the system's status and make informed decisions.

6.3.22 Question: What is a call-to-action (CTA) in interface design?
Answer: A CTA is a prompt that encourages users to take a specific action, such as signing up or making a purchase, typically using buttons or links.

6.3.23 Question: What is skeuomorphism in interface design?
Answer: Skeuomorphism is a design approach that mimics real-world objects and textures in digital interfaces to make them more familiar and intuitive.

6.3.24 Question: What is flat design?
Answer: Flat design is a minimalist design approach that emphasizes simplicity and usability, using clean, open space, and flat elements without gradients or textures.

6.3.25 Question: What is a navigation menu?
Answer: A navigation menu is a set of links or buttons that allow users to move between different sections or pages of a system.

6.3.26 Question: What is a user flow?
Answer: A user flow is a diagram that shows the steps a user takes to complete a specific task within the system, helping to design intuitive pathways.

6.3.27 Question: What is progressive disclosure?
Answer: Progressive disclosure is a design technique that presents only the necessary information upfront and reveals more details as needed, reducing cognitive load.

6.3.28 Question: What is the importance of whitespace in interface design?
Answer: Whitespace, or negative space, enhances readability and focus by separating elements and preventing the interface from appearing cluttered.

6.3.29 Question: What is micro interaction?
Answer: Micro interactions are small, task-based interactions that enhance user experience by providing feedback, such as liking a post or turning on a switch.

6.3.30 Question: What is the role of typography in interface design?
Answer: Typography involves the selection and arrangement of fonts and text to ensure readability, hierarchy, and aesthetic appeal in the user interface.

6.4 Design Patterns

6.4.1 Question: What are design patterns?
Answer: Design patterns are reusable solutions to common software design problems, providing templates to solve issues in a consistent and efficient manner.

6.4.2 Question: Why are design patterns important?
Answer: Design patterns are important because they provide proven solutions, enhance code readability, facilitate communication among developers, and improve software maintainability.

6.4.3 Question: What is the Singleton pattern?
Answer: The Singleton pattern ensures a class has only one instance and provides a global point of access to that instance.

6.4.4 Question: When would you use the Factory Method pattern?
Answer: The Factory Method pattern is used when a class cannot anticipate the type of objects it needs to create, and delegates the instantiation process to subclasses.

6.4.5 Question: What is the purpose of the Observer pattern?
Answer: The Observer pattern defines a one-to-many dependency between objects so that when one object changes state, all its dependents are notified and updated automatically.

6.4.6 Question: Can you explain the Strategy pattern?
Answer: The Strategy pattern defines a family of algorithms, encapsulates each one, and makes them interchangeable, allowing the algorithm to vary independently from clients that use it.

6.4.7 Question: What is the Decorator pattern used for?
Answer: The Decorator pattern is used to add new functionality to an object dynamically without altering its structure.

6.4.8 Question: How does the Adapter pattern work?
Answer: The Adapter pattern allows incompatible interfaces to work together by converting the interface of a class into another interface expected by clients.

6.4.9 Question: What is the Command pattern?
Answer: The Command pattern encapsulates a request as an object, thereby allowing parameterization of clients with queues, requests, and operations.

6.4.10 Question: What problem does the Proxy pattern solve?
Answer: The Proxy pattern provides a surrogate or placeholder for another object to control access to it, often used for lazy initialization, logging, or access control.

6.4.11 Question: What is the difference between the Prototype and Factory Method patterns?
Answer: The Prototype pattern creates objects by cloning an existing object, while the Factory Method pattern creates objects using a method in a class hierarchy.

6.4.12 Question: Can you describe the Chain of Responsibility pattern?
Answer: The Chain of Responsibility pattern passes a request along a chain of handlers, where each handler processes the request or passes it to the next handler in the chain.

6.4.13 Question: What is the main benefit of the Builder pattern?
Answer: The Builder pattern separates the construction of a complex object from its representation, allowing the same construction process to create different representations.

6.4.14 Question: How does the State pattern work?
Answer: The State pattern allows an object to alter its behaviour when its internal state changes, appearing to change its class.

6.4.15 Question: What is the Memento pattern used for?
Answer: The Memento pattern captures and externalizes an object's internal state without violating encapsulation, allowing the object to be restored to this state later.

6.4.16 Question: What is the role of the Composite pattern?

Answer: The Composite pattern composes objects into tree structures to represent part-whole hierarchies, allowing clients to treat individual objects and compositions uniformly.

6.4.17 Question: What is the Flyweight pattern?

Answer: The Flyweight pattern reduces the cost of creating and manipulating a large number of similar objects by sharing common parts of the state between multiple objects.

6.4.18 Question: How does the Iterator pattern enhance collections?

Answer: The Iterator pattern provides a way to access elements of a collection sequentially without exposing its underlying representation.

6.4.19 Question: What is the Template Method pattern?

Answer: The Template Method pattern defines the skeleton of an algorithm in a method, deferring some steps to subclasses, allowing them to redefine certain steps of the algorithm without changing its structure.

6.4.20 Question: Can you explain the Mediator pattern?

Answer: The Mediator pattern reduces the complexity of communication between multiple objects by centralizing their interactions through a mediator object.

6.4.21 Question: What is the purpose of the Visitor pattern?

Answer: The Visitor pattern separates an algorithm from the objects on which it operates, allowing new operations to be added without modifying the objects.

6.4.22 Question: What is the Bridge pattern?

Answer: The Bridge pattern decouples an abstraction from its implementation so that the two can vary independently, improving flexibility and scalability.

6.4.23 Question: What is the Interpreter pattern used for?

Answer: The Interpreter pattern defines a representation for a language's grammar and an interpreter that uses this representation to interpret sentences in the language.

6.4.24 Question: How does the Facade pattern simplify interactions?

Answer: The Facade pattern provides a unified interface to a set of interfaces in a subsystem, making it easier to use and reducing complexity for clients.

6.4.25 Question: What is the purpose of the Template Method pattern?

Answer: The Template Method pattern defines the basic steps of an algorithm and allows subclasses to redefine certain steps without changing the algorithm's structure.

6.4.26 Question: What problem does the Visitor pattern solve?

Answer: The Visitor pattern allows you to add further operations to objects without having to modify them, promoting the Open/Closed Principle.

6.4.27 Question: What is the difference between the Adapter and Bridge patterns?

Answer: The Adapter pattern changes the interface of an existing object, while the Bridge pattern separates an abstraction from its implementation to allow both to vary independently.

6.4.28 Question: When would you use the Chain of Responsibility pattern?

Answer: Use the Chain of Responsibility pattern when multiple objects might handle a request, and you want to decouple the sender and receiver by passing the request along a chain of potential handlers.

6.4.29 Question: How does the Flyweight pattern improve performance?

Answer: The Flyweight pattern improves performance by sharing as much data as possible with similar objects, reducing memory usage.

6.4.30 Question: What is the key benefit of the Prototype pattern?
Answer: The key benefit of the Prototype pattern is that it allows you to create new objects by copying existing ones, facilitating object creation and reducing overhead.

6.5 Security Design Considerations

6.5.1 Question: What is security design in system analysis and design?
Answer: Security design involves planning and implementing measures to protect systems from threats and vulnerabilities, ensuring data integrity, confidentiality, and availability.

6.5.2 Question: Why is security important in system design?
Answer: Security is crucial to protect sensitive data, maintain user trust, comply with regulations, and prevent financial and reputational damage caused by breaches.

6.5.3 Question: What are the key principles of security design?
Answer: Key principles include least privilege, defence in depth, security by design, and fail-safe defaults, which help minimize vulnerabilities and enhance protection.

6.5.4 Question: What is the principle of least privilege?
Answer: The principle of least privilege ensures that users and systems have the minimum access necessary to perform their tasks, reducing the risk of unauthorized access.

6.5.5 Question: What is defences in depth?
Answer: Defence in depth is a layered security approach that employs multiple security measures to protect systems, ensuring that if one layer fails, others still provide protection.

6.5.6 Question: What is security by design?
Answer: Security by design involves integrating security considerations into every phase of the system development lifecycle, from planning to deployment.

6.5.7 Question: What are fail-safe defaults?
Answer: Fail-safe defaults ensure that systems default to a secure state in case of failure, minimizing the risk of exposure or compromise.

6.5.8 Question: What is authentication?
Answer: Authentication is the process of verifying the identity of a user or system, ensuring that only authorized entities can access resources.

6.5.9 Question: What is authorization?
Answer: Authorization determines what resources and actions an authenticated user or system is permitted to access, based on predefined policies.

6.5.10 Question: What is encryption?
Answer: Encryption is the process of converting data into a coded format to prevent unauthorized access, ensuring data confidentiality and integrity during storage and transmission.

6.5.11 Question: What is a firewall?
Answer: A firewall is a network security device or software that monitors and controls incoming and outgoing network traffic based on predetermined security rules.

6.5.12 Question: What is intrusion detection and prevention?
Answer: Intrusion detection systems (IDS) and intrusion prevention systems (IPS) monitor network traffic for suspicious activity and take action to block or mitigate threats.

6.5.13 Question: What is a security policy?

Answer: A security policy is a formal set of rules and guidelines that define how an organization protects its information assets and responds to security incidents.

6.5.14 Question: What is risk assessment in security design?
Answer: Risk assessment involves identifying, evaluating, and prioritizing potential security risks to a system, informing the design of appropriate countermeasures.

6.5.15 Question: What is multi-factor authentication (MFA)?
Answer: MFA is a security mechanism that requires users to provide two or more verification factors, enhancing the security of the authentication process.

6.5.16 Question: What is a security audit?
Answer: A security audit is a systematic evaluation of a system's security measures, policies, and procedures to identify weaknesses and ensure compliance with standards.

6.5.17 Question: What is data integrity?
Answer: Data integrity ensures that information is accurate, consistent, and unaltered during storage and transmission, preventing unauthorized modifications.

6.5.18 Question: What is a security breach?
Answer: A security breach is an incident where unauthorized access to data, applications, services, networks, or devices occurs, potentially compromising information.

6.5.19 Question: What is vulnerability management?
Answer: Vulnerability management involves identifying, assessing, and mitigating security vulnerabilities in a system to reduce the risk of exploitation.

6.5.20 Question: What is the role of encryption in protecting data at rest?
Answer: Encryption protects data at rest by converting it into a secure format, ensuring that even if unauthorized access occurs, the data remains unreadable without the decryption key.

Online Resources

More Practices Questions

Online Exam Paper

URL
https://forms.gle/fUUtrZQoSiUE2Q4D7

QR Code

YouTube Video Playlist Link

Chapter 6

URL

https://www.youtube.com/playlist?list=PLzlh_31VWEFq63LVtoV5HlRcMPQHof7JA

QR Code

Chapter 7: Development Methodologies

7.1 Waterfall Model

7.1.1 Question: What is the Waterfall Model in system development?
Answer: The Waterfall Model is a linear and sequential approach to software development where each phase must be completed before the next one begins.

7.1.2 Question: What are the phases of the Waterfall Model?
Answer: The phases include Requirements, Design, Implementation, Verification, and Maintenance.

7.1.3 Question: Why is it called the Waterfall Model?
Answer: It is called the Waterfall Model because the process flows steadily downwards like a waterfall through the phases of software development.

7.1.4 Question: What is the main advantage of the Waterfall Model?
Answer: The main advantage is its simplicity and ease of management due to its linear structure.

7.1.5 Question: What is a major disadvantage of the Waterfall Model?
Answer: A major disadvantage is its inflexibility, as it is difficult to go back to a previous phase once it has been completed.

7.1.6 Question: In what type of projects is the Waterfall Model most suitable?
Answer: It is most suitable for projects with well-defined requirements and low risk of requirement changes.

7.1.7 Question: How does the Waterfall Model handle changes in requirements?
Answer: The Waterfall Model handles changes poorly, as any change requires a return to an earlier phase, which can be costly and time-consuming.

7.1.8 Question: What is the role of documentation in the Waterfall Model?
Answer: Documentation is crucial in the Waterfall Model as it provides a clear plan and ensures each phase is completed thoroughly before moving on.

7.1.9 Question: What happens during the Requirements phase?
Answer: In the Requirements phase, all system requirements are gathered and documented to provide a clear understanding of what needs to be built.

7.1.10 Question: What is the focus of the Design phase in the Waterfall Model?
Answer: The Design phase focuses on creating the architecture of the system, including both high-level design and detailed design.

7.1.11 Question: What activities are performed in the Implementation phase?
Answer: During the Implementation phase, the actual code is written based on the design documents.

7.1.12 Question: How is testing handled in the Waterfall Model?
Answer: Testing is conducted during the Verification phase, where the system is tested against the requirements to ensure it meets all specified criteria.

7.1.13 Question: What is the purpose of the Maintenance phase?
Answer: The Maintenance phase involves making updates and improvements to the system after deployment to fix bugs, improve performance, and adapt to changes.

7.1.14 Question: How does the Waterfall Model ensure quality?

Answer: Quality is ensured through rigorous documentation, predefined phases, and thorough testing in the Verification phase.

7.1.15 Question: Can the Waterfall Model be used in Agile environments?
Answer: Generally, the Waterfall Model is not suitable for Agile environments due to its rigid structure and sequential approach.

7.1.16 Question: What is a common use case for the Waterfall Model?
Answer: It is commonly used in projects with clear, fixed requirements and minimal changes, such as government or military projects.

7.1.17 Question: How does the Waterfall Model compare to Agile methodologies?
Answer: The Waterfall Model is linear and sequential, while Agile methodologies are iterative and incremental, allowing for more flexibility and adaptability.

7.1.18 Question: What is the importance of the Verification phase?
Answer: The Verification phase is crucial as it ensures that the system meets all the specified requirements and functions correctly before deployment.

7.1.19 Question: How does the Waterfall Model handle risk management?
Answer: Risk management is less flexible in the Waterfall Model since risks are addressed at the beginning, and changes are hard to implement later.

7.1.20 Question: What is the impact of late discovery of errors in the Waterfall Model?
Answer: Discovering errors late in the process can be very costly and time-consuming, as it may require returning to earlier phases to fix the issues.

7.1.21 Question: What kind of projects should avoid using the Waterfall Model?
Answer: Projects with high uncertainty, frequent requirement changes, or a need for early prototypes should avoid using the Waterfall Model.

7.1.22 Question: How does the Waterfall Model ensure project timeline adherence?
Answer: The sequential nature and detailed planning in the Waterfall Model help in adhering to project timelines.

7.1.23 Question: What is a critical path in the context of the Waterfall Model?
Answer: The critical path is the longest sequence of tasks in a project, determining the shortest time to complete the project.

7.1.24 Question: How does the Waterfall Model affect stakeholder involvement?
Answer: Stakeholder involvement is typically high at the beginning (Requirements phase) but minimal during later phases, except for review and feedback sessions.

7.1.25 Question: How does the Waterfall Model approach system deployment?
Answer: System deployment occurs only after the Verification phase is completed, ensuring the system is fully tested and validated before going live.

7.1.26 Question: What is the significance of milestone reviews in the Waterfall Model?
Answer: Milestone reviews ensure each phase is completed successfully before moving on, helping to maintain project quality and schedule.

7.1.27 Question: How does the Waterfall Model ensure team coordination?
Answer: Clear phase transitions and documentation help in coordinating team efforts and ensuring everyone is aligned with the project goals.

7.1.28 Question: How are dependencies managed in the Waterfall Model?

Answer: Dependencies are managed through detailed planning and sequential progression, ensuring that each phase builds on the previous one.

7.1.29 Question: How does the Waterfall Model handle large-scale projects?
Answer: The Waterfall Model can handle large-scale projects by breaking them into manageable phases and ensuring each phase is thoroughly documented and reviewed.

7.1.30 Question: What is the role of project management in the Waterfall Model?
Answer: Project management involves planning, executing, and monitoring each phase, ensuring the project stays on track and meets its objectives.

7.1.31 Question: How does the Waterfall Model handle integration testing?
Answer: Integration testing is conducted after the Implementation phase, where individual components are integrated and tested as a complete system.

7.1.32 Question: What is the impact of poor requirement analysis in the Waterfall Model?
Answer: Poor requirement analysis can lead to significant issues later, as changes are difficult to implement once the project progresses to later phases.

7.1.33 Question: How does the Waterfall Model ensure documentation quality?
Answer: Each phase produces detailed documentation, ensuring clarity and consistency throughout the project, which aids in future maintenance and updates.

7.1.34 Question: What is the significance of the Design phase in the Waterfall Model?
Answer: The Design phase is critical as it outlines the system architecture and detailed design, serving as the blueprint for the Implementation phase.

7.1.35 Question: How does the Waterfall Model address user feedback?
Answer: User feedback is typically gathered during the Requirements phase and reviewed during milestone checks, but incorporating changes can be challenging after the project progresses.

7.2 Agile Methodologies

7.2.1 Question: What is Agile methodology?
Answer: Agile methodology is an iterative and incremental approach to software development that emphasizes flexibility, collaboration, customer feedback, and rapid delivery of functional software.

7.2.2 Question: Can you explain the key principles of Agile?
Answer: Agile principles include customer satisfaction through early and continuous delivery, welcoming changing requirements, frequent delivery of working software, and close cooperation between business stakeholders and developers.

7.2.3 Question: What is a Scrum in Agile?
Answer: Scrum is a framework within Agile methodology that uses fixed-length iterations called sprints, typically lasting 2-4 weeks, to deliver incremental improvements to the product.

7.2.4 Question: What is a sprint in Scrum?
Answer: A sprint is a time-boxed period, usually 2-4 weeks, during which a specific set of work must be completed and made ready for review in the Scrum framework.

7.2.5 Question: Who are the key roles in a Scrum team?
Answer: The key roles in a Scrum team include the Product Owner, Scrum Master, and Development Team.

7.2.6 Question: What is the role of a Product Owner?
Answer: The Product Owner is responsible for defining product features, prioritizing the product backlog, and ensuring that the team delivers value to the business.

7.2.7 Question: What is the role of a Scrum Master?
Answer: The Scrum Master facilitates Scrum practices, removes impediments, and ensures the team follows Agile principles and practices.

7.2.8 Question: What is a product backlog?
Answer: The product backlog is an ordered list of all desired work on the project, managed and prioritized by the Product Owner.

7.2.9 Question: What is a sprint backlog?
Answer: The sprint backlog is a list of tasks identified by the Scrum team to be completed during the current sprint, derived from the product backlog.

7.2.10 Question: What is a daily stand-up meeting?
Answer: A daily stand-up meeting is a short, time-boxed meeting where team members discuss their progress, plans for the day, and any impediments they face.

7.2.11 Question: What is a sprint review?
Answer: A sprint review is a meeting held at the end of a sprint to inspect the increment and adapt the product backlog if needed.

7.2.12 Question: What is a sprint retrospective?
Answer: A sprint retrospective is a meeting held after the sprint review to reflect on the sprint process and identify areas for improvement.

7.2.13 Question: What is a user story?
Answer: A user story is a short, simple description of a feature from the perspective of the end user, used to capture product requirements in Agile.

7.2.14 Question: What is a story point?
Answer: A story point is a unit of measure used to estimate the relative effort needed to implement a user story in Agile.

7.2.15 Question: What is velocity in Agile?
Answer: Velocity is a metric that measures the amount of work a team can complete in a sprint, used to predict future performance.

7.2.16 Question: What is a burndown chart?
Answer: A burndown chart is a graphical representation showing the remaining work in the sprint backlog over time, used to track progress.

7.2.17 Question: What is a burnup chart?
Answer: A burnup chart is a graphical representation showing the amount of work completed and the total amount of work in a project, used to track progress.

7.2.18 Question: What is continuous integration?
Answer: Continuous integration is a practice where developers frequently integrate their code changes into a shared repository, followed by automated builds and tests.

7.2.19 Question: What is continuous delivery?
Answer: Continuous delivery is an extension of continuous integration that ensures code changes are automatically tested and prepared for release to production.

7.2.20 Question: What is Test-Driven Development (TDD)?
Answer: TDD is a software development approach where tests are written before the code itself, ensuring that the code meets the test criteria.

7.2.21 Question: What is pair programming?
Answer: Pair programming is a practice where two developers work together at one workstation, with one writing code and the other reviewing it simultaneously.

7.2.22 Question: What is the Agile Manifesto?
Answer: The Agile Manifesto is a declaration of four key values and twelve principles that guide Agile practices, emphasizing individuals and interactions, working software, customer collaboration, and responding to change.

7.2.23 Question: How does Agile handle changing requirements?
Answer: Agile welcomes changing requirements, even late in development, using iterative development and continuous feedback to adapt to changes.

7.2.24 Question: What is the difference between Agile and Waterfall methodologies?
Answer: Agile is iterative and flexible, focusing on continuous delivery and customer feedback, while Waterfall is linear and sequential, with distinct phases and less flexibility for changes.

7.2.25 Question: What is Kanban in Agile?
Answer: Kanban is an Agile framework that focuses on visualizing work, limiting work in progress, and improving flow by managing and optimizing the process.

7.2.26 Question: What are Agile artifacts?
Answer: Agile artifacts are key deliverables used in the Agile process, including the product backlog, sprint backlog, and increments.

7.2.27 Question: What is a definition of done?
Answer: The definition of done is a shared understanding within the team of what it means for work to be complete, ensuring consistency and quality.

7.2.28 Question: What is a release planning meeting?
Answer: A release planning meeting is held to define and plan the scope of work for a product release, including prioritization and estimation of features.

7.2.29 Question: What is an epic in Agile?
Answer: An epic is a large user story that can be broken down into smaller, more manageable stories, used to capture high-level requirements.

7.2.30 Question: What is backlog grooming?
Answer: Backlog grooming, or backlog refinement, is an ongoing process of reviewing and prioritizing the product backlog to ensure it is up-to-date and ready for future sprints.

7.2.31 Question: What is the role of a Development Team in Scrum?
Answer: The Development Team is responsible for delivering potentially shippable increments of the product at the end of each sprint, working collaboratively and self-organizing.

7.2.32 Question: What is a spike in Agile?
Answer: A spike is a time-boxed effort to research or investigate an issue or a solution, used to gain the knowledge necessary to reduce uncertainty in the project.

7.2.33 Question: What is Agile modelling?
Answer: Agile modelling is a practice that involves creating and using models to facilitate communication, understanding, and planning within an Agile project.

7.2.34 Question: What is Lean in Agile?

Answer: Lean is an Agile approach focused on delivering maximum value by eliminating waste, improving flow, and continuously enhancing processes and products.

7.2.35 Question: How does Agile promote collaboration?
Answer: Agile promotes collaboration through practices like daily stand-ups, sprint reviews, retrospectives, and close communication between team members and stakeholders.

7.3 DevOps Practices

7.3.1 Question: What is DevOps?
Answer: DevOps is a set of practices that combines software development (Dev) and IT operations (Ops) to shorten the development lifecycle and deliver high-quality software continuously.

7.3.2 Question: Why is DevOps important in modern software development?
Answer: DevOps is important because it enhances collaboration between development and operations teams, accelerates software delivery, improves deployment frequency, and increases the reliability of applications.

7.3.3 Question: What are the key principles of DevOps?
Answer: The key principles of DevOps include continuous integration, continuous delivery, infrastructure as code, monitoring and logging, and collaboration and communication.

7.3.4 Question: Can you explain Continuous Integration (CI)?
Answer: Continuous Integration (CI) is a DevOps practice where developers frequently integrate code into a shared repository, allowing automated builds and tests to detect errors early in the development process.

7.3.5 Question: What is Continuous Delivery (CD)?
Answer: Continuous Delivery (CD) is a practice where code changes are automatically built, tested, and prepared for release to production, ensuring that software can be reliably released at any time.

7.3.6 Question: How does Infrastructure as Code (IaC) benefit DevOps?
Answer: IaC allows the management and provisioning of infrastructure through code, making it easier to replicate environments, reduce errors, and ensure consistency across deployments.

7.3.7 Question: What tools are commonly used in DevOps for CI/CD?
Answer: Common tools include Jenkins, GitLab CI, Travis CI, CircleCI for CI, and Docker, Kubernetes, Ansible for CD and infrastructure automation.

7.3.8 Question: How do monitoring and logging support DevOps practices?
Answer: Monitoring and logging provide visibility into application performance and system health, enabling teams to detect, diagnose, and resolve issues quickly, thus maintaining reliability and performance.

7.3.9 Question: What is the role of automation in DevOps?
Answer: Automation in DevOps streamlines repetitive tasks, reduces human error, speeds up processes, and ensures consistent and reliable software delivery.

7.3.10 Question: How does DevOps improve collaboration between teams?
Answer: DevOps fosters a culture of collaboration and shared responsibility by encouraging frequent communication, integrating development and operations workflows, and aligning goals across teams.

7.3.11 Question: What is the significance of version control in DevOps?
Answer: Version control systems, such as Git, allow teams to track changes, collaborate efficiently, manage code versions, and maintain a history of modifications, which is crucial for CI/CD practices.

7.3.12 Question: What is a DevOps pipeline?
Answer: A DevOps pipeline automates the processes involved in software delivery, including coding, building, testing, deploying, and monitoring, ensuring smooth and continuous delivery.

7.3.13 Question: Can you explain the concept of "shift left" in DevOps?
Answer: "Shift left" in DevOps means integrating testing and quality checks earlier in the development process to detect and fix issues sooner, leading to higher quality and faster delivery.

7.3.14 Question: What is containerization and how does it relate to DevOps?
Answer: Containerization involves packaging an application and its dependencies into a container, such as Docker, ensuring consistency across different environments and simplifying deployment and scaling.

7.3.15 Question: How does DevOps support agile methodologies?
Answer: DevOps complements agile methodologies by promoting iterative development, continuous feedback, and quick releases, enhancing the overall flexibility and responsiveness of the development process.

7.4 Choosing the Right Methodology

7.4.1 Question: What factors should be considered when choosing a development methodology?
Answer: Consider factors such as project size, complexity, timeline, team skills, client requirements, and flexibility needed in the development process.

7.4.2 Question: What is the Agile methodology?
Answer: Agile is an iterative and incremental approach to software development emphasizing flexibility, collaboration, and customer feedback.

7.4.3 Question: What is the Waterfall model?
Answer: The Waterfall model is a linear and sequential approach where each phase must be completed before the next begins, suitable for well-defined projects.

7.4.4 Question: What is the Spiral model?
Answer: The Spiral model combines iterative development with systematic aspects of the Waterfall model, focusing on risk assessment and mitigation.

7.4.5 Question: What is Scrum?
Answer: Scrum is an Agile framework that divides projects into small iterations called sprints, emphasizing collaboration, flexibility, and continuous improvement.

7.4.6 Question: What is coupling in software engineering?
Answer: Coupling refers to the degree of interdependence between software modules; low coupling is desirable as it indicates modules are independent.

7.4.7 Question: What is cohesion in software engineering?
Answer: Cohesion refers to the degree to which elements of a module belong together; high cohesion is desirable as it indicates a single, well-defined purpose.

7.4.8 Question: How are coupling and cohesion related?
Answer: Ideally, software design aims for low coupling and high cohesion, making modules independent and focused, thus improving maintainability and flexibility.

7.4.9 Question: What is a Decision Support System (DSS)?
Answer: A DSS is an information system that supports business or organizational decision-making activities, using data, models, and analysis tools.

7.4.10 Question: What are the components of a Decision Support System?
Answer: Components include a database, model base, user interface, and the DSS software system that integrates these components.

7.4.11 Question: What is object-oriented programming (OOP)?

Answer: OOP is a programming paradigm based on the concept of objects, which contain data and methods, promoting reuse, modularity, and abstraction.

7.4.12 Question: What are the four main principles of OOP?
Answer: The four main principles are encapsulation, inheritance, polymorphism, and abstraction.

7.4.13 Question: What is encapsulation in OOP?
Answer: Encapsulation is the concept of bundling data and methods that operate on the data within a single unit or class, restricting direct access to some components.

7.4.14 Question: What is inheritance in OOP?
Answer: Inheritance allows a class to inherit properties and methods from another class, promoting code reuse and hierarchical relationships.

7.4.15 Question: What is polymorphism in OOP?
Answer: Polymorphism allows objects to be treated as instances of their parent class rather than their actual class, enabling a single interface to represent different underlying forms.

7.4.16 Question: What is abstraction in OOP?
Answer: Abstraction is the concept of hiding the complex implementation details and showing only the essential features of an object.

7.4.17 Question: What is a class in OOP?
Answer: A class is a blueprint for creating objects, defining attributes and methods that the objects created from the class will have.

7.4.18 Question: What is an object in OOP?
Answer: An object is an instance of a class, containing data and behaviour defined by the class.

7.4.19 Question: What is UML?
Answer: UML (Unified Modelling Language) is a standardized modelling language used to visualize, specify, construct, and document the artifacts of software systems.

7.4.20 Question: What is a use case diagram in UML?
Answer: A use case diagram shows the interactions between users (actors) and the system, representing functional requirements.

7.4.21 Question: What is a class diagram in UML?
Answer: A class diagram shows the static structure of a system, illustrating classes, attributes, operations, and relationships among objects.

7.4.22 Question: What is a sequence diagram in UML?
Answer: A sequence diagram illustrates how objects interact in a particular scenario of a use case, showing the sequence of messages exchanged.

7.4.23 Question: What is a state diagram in UML?
Answer: A state diagram shows the states of an object and transitions between these states in response to events.

7.4.24 Question: What is a component diagram in UML?
Answer: A component diagram shows the organization and dependencies among software components.

7.4.25 Question: What is a deployment diagram in UML?
Answer: A deployment diagram shows the physical deployment of artifacts on nodes, depicting the hardware and software components.

7.4.26 Question: What is the importance of design patterns in OOP?
Answer: Design patterns provide reusable solutions to common design problems, promoting best practices and improving code maintainability and scalability.

7.4.27 Question: What is the Singleton pattern?
Answer: The Singleton pattern ensures a class has only one instance and provides a global point of access to it.

7.4.28 Question: What is the Factory pattern?
Answer: The Factory pattern provides an interface for creating objects without specifying the exact class of the object that will be created.

7.4.29 Question: What is the Observer pattern?
Answer: The Observer pattern defines a one-to-many dependency between objects, so when one object changes state, all its dependents are notified and updated automatically.

7.4.30 Question: What is the Adapter pattern?
Answer: The Adapter pattern allows incompatible interfaces to work together by converting the interface of a class into another interface the client expects.

7.4.31 Question: What is the purpose of a Decision Support System in business?
Answer: A DSS aids in decision-making by providing relevant data, analytical models, and tools to analyse business problems and support informed decision-making.

7.4.32 Question: What is the difference between DSS and MIS?
Answer: DSS supports complex decision-making and problem-solving, while MIS (Management Information System) focuses on routine data processing and reporting for management.

7.4.33 Question: How does cohesion affect software design?
Answer: High cohesion within modules ensures that they are focused and easier to maintain, leading to more reliable and understandable software.

7.4.34 Question: Why is low coupling desirable in software design?
Answer: Low coupling reduces dependencies between modules, making the system more modular, easier to understand, and less prone to errors during modifications.

7.4.35 Question: What is a methodology in system development?
Answer: A methodology is a structured approach to planning, developing, and maintaining information systems, encompassing models, techniques, and tools to achieve project goals.

Online Resources

More Practices Questions

Online Exam Paper
URL
https://forms.gle/ed8yEpsi8B3V7yLe9
QR Code

YouTube Video Playlist Link

Chapter 7
URL
https://www.youtube.com/playlist?list=PLzlh_31VWEFoqka19unBzSGpp5MN4yhg5
QR Code

Chapter 8: Implementation and Testing

8.1 Coding and Unit Testing

8.1.1 Question: What is the purpose of coding in system development?
Answer: Coding involves translating system design specifications into executable code using a programming language, creating the functional components of the system.

8.1.2 Question: What are coding standards?
Answer: Coding standards are guidelines that developers follow to write consistent, maintainable, and error-free code, promoting quality and uniformity across the project.

8.1.3 Question: What is unit testing?
Answer: Unit testing involves testing individual components or modules of the system in isolation to ensure they function correctly and meet their specifications.

8.1.4 Question: Why is unit testing important?
Answer: Unit testing is crucial as it helps identify and fix defects early in the development process, improving code quality and reducing the cost of fixing bugs later.

8.1.5 Question: What is a test case in unit testing?
Answer: A test case is a set of conditions or variables used to determine whether a system component functions correctly and meets its requirements.

8.1.6 Question: What is a test suite?
Answer: A test suite is a collection of test cases that are intended to be executed together to test a specific aspect of the system comprehensively.

8.1.7 Question: What tools are commonly used for unit testing?
Answer: Common unit testing tools include JUnit for Java, NUnit for .NET, and pytest for Python, which help automate and streamline the testing process.

8.1.8 Question: What is test-driven development (TDD)?
Answer: TDD is a software development approach where test cases are written before the code itself, guiding the coding process and ensuring thorough testing.

8.1.9 Question: What are mock objects in unit testing?
Answer: Mock objects simulate the behaviour of real objects in a controlled way, allowing testers to isolate the component under test and verify its interactions.

8.1.10 Question: What is code review?
Answer: Code review is the process of examining written code by other developers to identify defects, ensure adherence to coding standards, and improve overall code quality.

8.1.11 Question: How does continuous integration (CI) relate to unit testing?
Answer: CI involves automatically integrating and testing code changes frequently, ensuring that unit tests are run regularly to catch issues early and maintain code stability.

8.1.12 Question: What is refactoring in coding?
Answer: Refactoring is the process of restructuring existing code without changing its external behaviour to improve readability, reduce complexity, and enhance maintainability.

8.1.13 Question: What is a build in software development?
Answer: A build is a version of the software that has been compiled and linked, ready for testing or deployment, often generated automatically by a build system.

8.1.14 Question: What is the role of a build system?
Answer: A build system automates the process of compiling and linking code, running tests, and preparing the software for deployment, ensuring consistency and efficiency.

8.1.15 Question: What is code coverage in unit testing?
Answer: Code coverage measures the extent to which the code is executed during testing, indicating how thoroughly the code has been tested and identifying untested parts.

8.1.16 Question: What is a regression test?
Answer: Regression testing involves re-running previously conducted tests after code changes to ensure that existing functionality remains unaffected.

8.1.17 Question: What is an integration test?
Answer: Integration testing examines how different modules or components of the system work together, ensuring they integrate correctly and function as a whole.

8.1.18 Question: What is a system test?
Answer: System testing evaluates the complete and integrated system to verify that it meets specified requirements and performs as expected in a production-like environment.

8.1.19 Question: What is user acceptance testing (UAT)?
Answer: UAT involves testing the system by end-users to ensure it meets their needs and requirements, typically performed before the system goes live.

8.1.20 Question: What is a defect or bug in software testing?
Answer: A defect or bug is an error or flaw in the software that causes it to produce incorrect or unexpected results, deviating from its expected behaviour.

8.1.21 Question: What is the role of a tester in system development?
Answer: A tester is responsible for designing, executing, and evaluating tests to ensure the system functions correctly and meets specified requirements.

8.1.22 Question: What is the difference between black-box and white-box testing?
Answer: Black-box testing focuses on testing the system's functionality without considering its internal code structure, while white-box testing examines the internal workings and code logic.

8.1.23 Question: What is a testing framework?
Answer: A testing framework is a set of guidelines, tools, and practices used to create and manage tests, automate testing, and ensure consistent testing practices.

8.1.24 Question: What is the importance of automated testing?
Answer: Automated testing enhances efficiency and reliability by running tests automatically, reducing manual effort, and enabling frequent and consistent testing.

8.1.25 Question: What is exploratory testing?
Answer: Exploratory testing involves simultaneously learning, test design, and test execution, allowing testers to explore the system and identify issues based on their knowledge and intuition.

8.1.26 Question: What is a bug report?
Answer: A bug report documents a defect found during testing, providing details such as steps to reproduce, expected and actual results, and severity to help developers fix the issue.

8.1.27 Question: What is a test environment?
Answer: A test environment is a configured setup where tests are executed, including hardware, software, network configurations, and other necessary components.

8.1.28 Question: What is continuous testing?
Answer: Continuous testing involves integrating testing activities into the CI/CD pipeline, ensuring that tests are run automatically at each stage of development and deployment.

8.1.29 Question: What is a performance test?
Answer: Performance testing evaluates the system's responsiveness, stability, and scalability under various conditions, identifying bottlenecks and performance issues.

8.1.30 Question: What is a load test?
Answer: Load testing examines how the system performs under expected and peak load conditions, ensuring it can handle high user traffic and data processing.

8.1.31 Question: What is stress testing?
Answer: Stress testing assesses the system's behaviour under extreme conditions or beyond its specified limits, identifying breaking points and robustness.

8.1.32 Question: What is security testing?
Answer: Security testing evaluates the system's ability to protect data and maintain functionality against security threats and vulnerabilities.

8.1.33 Question: What is usability testing?
Answer: Usability testing assesses how easy and user-friendly the system is, involving real users to provide feedback on the interface and overall experience.

8.1.34 Question: What is the role of a version control system in coding?
Answer: A version control system manages changes to the codebase, enabling collaboration, tracking revisions, and maintaining a history of code changes.

8.1.35 Question: What is continuous deployment?
Answer: Continuous deployment automates the release process, deploying code changes to production environments automatically after passing tests, ensuring rapid and reliable updates

8.2 Integration Testing

8.2.1 Question: What is Integration Testing?
Answer: Integration testing is the phase in software testing where individual units or components are combined and tested as a group to identify any issues in their interaction.

8.2.2 Question: Why is Integration Testing important?
Answer: Integration testing is important because it ensures that combined components work together correctly and helps identify issues related to interface and data flow between modules.

8.2.3 Question: What are the different approaches to Integration Testing?
Answer: The main approaches to integration testing are Big Bang, Top-Down, Bottom-Up, and Hybrid (also known as Sandwich) testing.

8.2.4 Question: What is Big Bang Integration Testing?
Answer: Big Bang integration testing involves integrating all components at once and testing the entire system as a whole. It is simple but can make debugging difficult.

8.2.5 Question: What is Top-Down Integration Testing?
Answer: Top-Down integration testing starts with the highest-level modules and progressively integrates and tests lower-level modules using stubs for unfinished modules.

8.2.6 Question: What is Bottom-Up Integration Testing?

Answer: Bottom-Up integration testing starts with the lowest-level modules and progressively integrates and tests higher-level modules using drivers for unfinished modules.

8.2.7 Question: What is Hybrid Integration Testing?
Answer: Hybrid (or Sandwich) integration testing combines Top-Down and Bottom-Up approaches, testing from both the top and the bottom towards the middle.

8.2.8 Question: What are stubs and drivers in Integration Testing?
Answer: Stubs are dummy modules that simulate lower-level components, used in Top-Down testing. Drivers are dummy modules that simulate higher-level components, used in Bottom-Up testing.

8.2.9 Question: What is Incremental Integration Testing?
Answer: Incremental integration testing involves integrating and testing modules in small increments rather than all at once, making it easier to isolate and fix defects.

8.2.10 Question: What is Functional Integration Testing?
Answer: Functional integration testing focuses on testing the interactions between integrated modules to ensure they meet the specified functional requirements.

8.2.11 Question: What is Non-Functional Integration Testing?
Answer: Non-functional integration testing evaluates the system's performance, usability, reliability, and other non-functional aspects after integrating the modules.

8.2.12 Question: What is Continuous Integration?
Answer: Continuous integration is a development practice where code changes are automatically tested and integrated into the main branch frequently, often multiple times a day.

8.2.13 Question: What are the benefits of Continuous Integration?
Answer: Benefits of continuous integration include early detection of defects, reduced integration problems, improved code quality, and faster development cycles.

8.2.14 Question: What tools are commonly used for Integration Testing?
Answer: Common tools for integration testing include JUnit, NUnit, TestNG, Selenium, Jenkins, and Apache JMeter.

8.2.15 Question: What is the role of test data in Integration Testing?
Answer: Test data is crucial in integration testing to simulate real-world scenarios and ensure that integrated components function correctly under various conditions.

8.2.16 Question: How do you handle dependencies in Integration Testing?
Answer: Handling dependencies involves using stubs and drivers, creating mock objects, and ensuring that all necessary components are available and configured correctly.

8.2.17 Question: What are some common challenges in Integration Testing?
Answer: Common challenges include managing complex dependencies, ensuring adequate test coverage, handling large volumes of test data, and debugging integration issues.

8.2.18 Question: What is the difference between System Testing and Integration Testing?
Answer: System testing evaluates the complete system's functionality as a whole, while integration testing focuses on interactions and data flow between integrated modules.

8.2.19 Question: How do you prioritize test cases in Integration Testing?
Answer: Prioritizing test cases involves focusing on critical interfaces, high-risk areas, frequently used paths, and components with complex interactions.

8.2.20 Question: What is a Test Harness in Integration Testing?

Answer: A test harness is a collection of software and test data used to test modules in isolation by simulating inputs and recording outputs for comparison with expected results.

8.2.21 Question: What are the exit criteria for Integration Testing?
Answer: Exit criteria for integration testing include meeting predefined test coverage, passing all critical test cases, resolving major defects, and obtaining stakeholder approval.

8.2.22 Question: How does integration testing fit into the SDLC?
Answer: Integration testing is typically performed after unit testing and before system testing, ensuring that integrated components work together as expected within the system.

8.2.23 Question: What is Smoke Testing?
Answer: Smoke testing is a preliminary test to check the basic functionality of integrated components before proceeding with more detailed integration tests.

8.2.24 Question: What is Sanity Testing?
Answer: Sanity testing is a subset of regression testing focused on verifying specific functionality after minor changes to ensure that bugs have been fixed and no new issues have been introduced.

8.2.25 Question: How do you document Integration Test cases?
Answer: Documenting integration test cases involves detailing test scenarios, steps, expected results, actual results, and any discrepancies, ensuring traceability and repeatability.

8.3 Deployment Strategies

8.3.1 Question: What is deployment in the context of system analysis and design?
Answer: Deployment is the process of delivering the completed software to the user or client environment where it will be used.

8.3.2 Question: Can you explain the difference between deployment and release?
Answer: Deployment involves the technical activities to install and configure the software in the target environment, whereas release is the broader process that includes deployment, documentation, and communication to end-users.

8.3.3 Question: What is a deployment pipeline?
Answer: A deployment pipeline is an automated process that moves software from development through various stages of testing to production, ensuring quality and consistency.

8.3.4 Question: What is continuous deployment?
Answer: Continuous deployment is a practice where code changes are automatically deployed to production after passing automated tests, enabling rapid and reliable software updates.

8.3.5 Question: What are the key stages in a deployment pipeline?
Answer: Key stages include code commit, build, automated tests, staging environment, user acceptance testing, and production deployment.

8.3.6 Question: What is blue-green deployment?
Answer: Blue-green deployment is a strategy that reduces downtime and risk by running two identical production environments (blue and green) and switching traffic to the new version (green) once it's ready.

8.3.7 Question: What is canary deployment?
Answer: Canary deployment is a strategy where a new software version is gradually rolled out to a small subset of users before a full-scale release, minimizing the impact of potential issues.

8.3.8 Question: What is a rollback in deployment?

Answer: A rollback is the process of reverting to a previous stable version of the software in case of deployment issues or failures.

8.3.9 Question: What is the importance of monitoring in deployment?
Answer: Monitoring ensures that any issues or anomalies in the deployed software are quickly detected and addressed, maintaining system reliability and performance.

8.3.10 Question: What is A/B testing in deployment?
Answer: A/B testing involves deploying two versions of the software to different user groups to compare performance and user experience, helping to determine the best version.

8.3.11 Question: How does containerization help in deployment?
Answer: Containerization packages software with all its dependencies into containers, ensuring consistency across different environments and simplifying deployment.

8.3.12 Question: What is the role of configuration management in deployment?
Answer: Configuration management involves maintaining and managing the software and hardware configurations, ensuring consistency and compliance across deployment environments.

8.3.13 Question: What are deployment scripts?
Answer: Deployment scripts are automated scripts that perform tasks such as installation, configuration, and setup of software in the deployment environment.

8.3.14 Question: What is the purpose of a staging environment?
Answer: A staging environment is a replica of the production environment used for final testing before deployment, ensuring that the software works as expected.

8.3.15 Question: What are the challenges of deploying in a multi-cloud environment?
Answer: Challenges include managing different cloud platforms, ensuring interoperability, handling data synchronization, and maintaining consistent security practices.

8.3.16 Question: What is the importance of user acceptance testing (UAT) in deployment?
Answer: UAT involves real users testing the software in a staging environment to ensure it meets their needs and requirements before full deployment.

8.3.17 Question: What is the role of documentation in deployment?
Answer: Documentation provides detailed instructions and information about the deployment process, ensuring that team members can understand and execute deployment tasks accurately.

8.3.18 Question: How does DevOps culture impact deployment?
Answer: DevOps promotes collaboration between development and operations teams, streamlining the deployment process and improving software quality and delivery speed.

8.3.19 Question: What is zero-downtime deployment?
Answer: Zero-downtime deployment ensures that the software is updated without any interruption to the service, providing continuous availability to users.

8.3.20 Question: What are the benefits of using infrastructure as code (IaC) in deployment?
Answer: IaC automates the setup and management of infrastructure, ensuring consistency, reducing errors, and enabling version control.

8.3.21 Question: What is feature toggling in deployment?
Answer: Feature toggling allows new features to be turned on or off dynamically in the production environment, facilitating incremental releases and testing.

8.3.22 Question: What is a deployment checklist?

Answer: A deployment checklist is a predefined list of tasks and checks to ensure all necessary steps are completed for a successful deployment.

8.3.23 Question: How do you handle deployment dependencies?
Answer: Managing deployment dependencies involves identifying and coordinating the installation of all required components and services to ensure compatibility and functionality.

8.3.24 Question: What is post-deployment validation?
Answer: Post-deployment validation involves verifying that the deployed software operates as intended in the production environment, often through automated and manual tests.

8.3.25 Question: What is the role of security in deployment?
Answer: Security in deployment ensures that the software is protected against vulnerabilities and threats, implementing practices such as encryption, access control, and regular audits.

8.4 User Training and Acceptance Testing

8.4.1 Question: What is user training in system development?
Answer: User training involves educating end-users on how to effectively use the new system, ensuring they understand its functionalities and can operate it efficiently.

8.4.2 Question: Why is user training important?
Answer: User training is crucial because it helps users transition smoothly to the new system, reducing resistance and increasing productivity by ensuring they are competent and comfortable with the system.

8.4.3 Question: What are the different types of user training?
Answer: Types of user training include on-the-job training, classroom training, online training, workshops, and user manuals.

8.4.4 Question: What is acceptance testing?
Answer: Acceptance testing is a phase of system testing where the system is tested against user requirements to ensure it meets the specified criteria and is ready for deployment.

8.4.5 Question: Who conducts acceptance testing?
Answer: Acceptance testing is typically conducted by the end-users or clients to verify that the system meets their requirements and expectations.

8.4.6 Question: What are the objectives of acceptance testing?
Answer: The objectives of acceptance testing are to validate that the system functions as intended, meets user needs, and is ready for production use.

8.4.7 Question: What are the types of acceptance testing?
Answer: Types of acceptance testing include user acceptance testing (UAT), operational acceptance testing (OAT), and contract acceptance testing (CAT).

8.4.8 Question: What is user acceptance testing (UAT)?
Answer: UAT is a type of acceptance testing where end-users test the system to ensure it meets their business requirements and works in real-world scenarios.

8.4.9 Question: What is operational acceptance testing (OAT)?
Answer: OAT is a type of acceptance testing that verifies if the system meets the operational requirements and can be supported in the production environment.

8.4.10 Question: What is contract acceptance testing (CAT)?
Answer: CAT is a type of acceptance testing that ensures the system meets the contractual obligations and specifications agreed upon between the client and the vendor.

8.4.11 Question: What is the role of a test plan in acceptance testing?
Answer: A test plan outlines the scope, approach, resources, and schedule for the testing activities, ensuring all aspects of the system are adequately tested.

8.4.12 Question: How do you prepare for user training?
Answer: Preparation for user training involves developing training materials, scheduling training sessions, and ensuring trainers are well-versed in the system functionalities.

8.4.13 Question: What are the key components of a user training program?
Answer: Key components include training objectives, course content, training materials, delivery methods, and evaluation criteria.

8.4.14 Question: What are some effective user training methods?
Answer: Effective methods include hands-on training, interactive workshops, e-learning modules, and detailed user manuals.

8.4.15 Question: How do you evaluate the effectiveness of user training?
Answer: Effectiveness can be evaluated through user feedback, performance assessments, and measuring improvements in user competence and productivity.

8.4.16 Question: What is a training needs analysis?
Answer: A training needs analysis identifies the skills and knowledge gaps among users to design a training program that addresses their specific needs.

8.4.17 Question: What are the challenges in user training?
Answer: Challenges include resistance to change, varying levels of user expertise, scheduling conflicts, and ensuring the training content is relevant and up-to-date.

8.4.18 Question: How can you overcome resistance to user training?
Answer: Overcoming resistance involves clear communication of the benefits, involving users early in the process, and providing continuous support and encouragement.

8.4.19 Question: What is the significance of a user manual?
Answer: A user manual provides detailed instructions and information about the system, serving as a reference guide for users to troubleshoot and operate the system effectively.

8.4.20 Question: What is the role of feedback in user training?
Answer: Feedback helps in improving the training program by identifying areas of improvement and ensuring that user concerns and suggestions are addressed.

8.4.21 Question: What is pilot testing?
Answer: Pilot testing involves implementing the system in a limited scope to identify any issues and gather user feedback before full-scale deployment.

8.4.22 Question: What is the purpose of a training session evaluation?
Answer: Training session evaluations assess the effectiveness of the training, providing insights into what worked well and what needs improvement.

8.4.23 Question: How do you ensure continuous learning post-training?
Answer: Continuous learning can be ensured through follow-up sessions, refresher courses, access to online resources, and ongoing support.

8.4.24 Question: What is the difference between formal and informal training?
Answer: Formal training is structured and planned with specific objectives, while informal training occurs spontaneously, often through on-the-job interactions and mentoring.

8.4.25 Question: What are acceptance criteria in acceptance testing?
Answer: Acceptance criteria are predefined conditions that the system must meet to be considered acceptable by the end-users or clients.

8.4.26 Question: What is the role of test cases in acceptance testing?
Answer: Test cases define specific conditions under which the system is tested, ensuring all functionalities and requirements are validated.

8.4.27 Question: How do you handle defects found during acceptance testing?
Answer: Defects are documented, prioritized, and communicated to the development team for resolution, followed by retesting to ensure they are fixed.

8.4.28 Question: What is a training schedule?
Answer: A training schedule outlines the timeline and sequence of training sessions, ensuring that all users receive the necessary training in a timely manner.

8.4.29 Question: What is user documentation?
Answer: User documentation includes all materials that help users understand and use the system effectively, such as user manuals, FAQs, and help guides.

8.4.30 Question: How do you measure user satisfaction after training?
Answer: User satisfaction can be measured through surveys, feedback forms, and interviews to gauge their comfort level and proficiency with the new system.

8.4.31 Question: What is the importance of scenario-based training?
Answer: Scenario-based training uses realistic scenarios to teach users how to handle specific situations, enhancing their problem-solving skills and preparedness.

8.4.32 Question: What are the common pitfalls in acceptance testing?
Answer: Common pitfalls include inadequate test planning, insufficient user involvement, and lack of clear acceptance criteria.

8.4.33 Question: How do you ensure training materials are effective?
Answer: Training materials should be clear, concise, and relevant, incorporating examples, visuals, and step-by-step instructions to aid understanding.

8.4.34 Question: What is the role of a trainer in user training?
Answer: A trainer facilitates the learning process, providing instruction, guidance, and support to help users understand and use the system effectively.

8.4.35 Question: How do you conduct a post-training evaluation?
Answer: Post-training evaluations involve collecting feedback, assessing user performance, and reviewing training outcomes to identify areas for improvement.

8.5 Software Maintenance Activities

8.5.1 Question: What is software maintenance?
Answer: Software maintenance is the process of modifying and updating software after its initial deployment to correct faults, improve performance, or adapt to a changed environment.

8.5.2 Question: What are the types of software maintenance?
Answer: The main types of software maintenance are corrective, adaptive, perfective, and preventive maintenance.

8.5.3 Question: What is corrective maintenance?

Answer: Corrective maintenance involves fixing bugs and errors discovered after the software has been deployed.

8.5.4 Question: What is adaptive maintenance?
Answer: Adaptive maintenance is the process of updating software to keep it compatible with changing environments, such as new operating systems or hardware.

8.5.5 Question: What is perfective maintenance?
Answer: Perfective maintenance includes enhancements and improvements to the software to add new features or optimize performance.

8.5.6 Question: What is preventive maintenance?
Answer: Preventive maintenance involves making changes to software to prevent future problems, improving its reliability and maintainability.

8.5.7 Question: Why is software maintenance important?
Answer: Software maintenance is crucial for ensuring the software remains functional, secure, and relevant to user needs over time.

8.5.8 Question: What is a software maintenance plan?
Answer: A software maintenance plan outlines the strategies, procedures, and resources needed for ongoing maintenance of the software.

8.5.9 Question: How do you prioritize maintenance tasks?
Answer: Maintenance tasks are prioritized based on factors such as severity of issues, user impact, and business goals.

8.5.10 Question: What role does documentation play in software maintenance?
Answer: Documentation provides detailed information about the software's design, functionality, and changes, aiding in efficient maintenance and troubleshooting.

8.5.11 Question: What is regression testing in software maintenance?
Answer: Regression testing involves retesting the software after changes to ensure that existing functionalities are not affected.

8.5.12 Question: How is user feedback used in software maintenance?
Answer: User feedback is collected and analysed to identify bugs, request features, and improve the overall user experience.

8.5.13 Question: What tools are commonly used for software maintenance?
Answer: Common tools include version control systems, debugging tools, testing frameworks, and issue tracking systems.

8.5.14 Question: How do you manage software updates?
Answer: Software updates are managed through a structured process that includes planning, development, testing, and deployment.

8.5.15 Question: What is the role of a maintenance team?
Answer: The maintenance team is responsible for identifying, prioritizing, and implementing changes to keep the software functional and up-to-date.

8.5.16 Question: What challenges are faced during software maintenance?
Answer: Challenges include managing legacy systems, handling complex dependencies, and ensuring minimal disruption to users during updates.

8.5.17 Question: What is the impact of poor maintenance on software?

Answer: Poor maintenance can lead to software becoming buggy, insecure, inefficient, and eventually obsolete.

8.5.18 Question: How does preventive maintenance differ from corrective maintenance?
Answer: Preventive maintenance focuses on preventing issues before they occur, while corrective maintenance deals with fixing issues after they have been identified.

8.5.19 Question: What is the importance of maintaining software compatibility?
Answer: Maintaining compatibility ensures that the software works correctly with new hardware, operating systems, and other dependent software.

8.5.20 Question: How does software maintenance contribute to software longevity?
Answer: Effective maintenance extends the lifespan of software by keeping it functional, secure, and aligned with user needs and technological advancements.

8.6 Bug Fixes and Patch Management

8.6.1 Question: What is a bug in software development?
Answer: A bug is an error, flaw, or fault in a software program that causes it to produce incorrect or unexpected results, or to behave in unintended ways.

8.6.2 Question: What is the purpose of patch management?
Answer: Patch management involves the process of acquiring, testing, and installing patches (updates) to fix bugs, improve performance, and enhance security in software systems.

8.6.3 Question: How do you prioritize bug fixes?
Answer: Bug fixes are prioritized based on their severity and impact on the system's functionality, user experience, and security, with critical bugs addressed first.

8.6.4 Question: What is a hotfix?
Answer: A hotfix is a quick and targeted software update released to fix a specific, critical issue without waiting for the next regular update cycle.

8.6.5 Question: What is regression testing in the context of bug fixes?
Answer: Regression testing involves re-running previously completed tests after a bug fix to ensure that the changes have not introduced new defects or broken existing functionality.

8.6.6 Question: How do you ensure a patch is safe to deploy?
Answer: Ensuring a patch is safe involves thorough testing in a controlled environment, reviewing the patch documentation, and following a structured deployment process to minimize risks.

8.6.7 Question: What is the difference between a patch and a release?
Answer: A patch is a small update intended to fix specific issues or vulnerabilities, while a release is a more comprehensive update that may include new features, enhancements, and multiple bug fixes.

8.6.8 Question: What role does version control play in patch management?
Answer: Version control systems track changes to the software code, helping manage and organize patches, ensuring that updates are applied consistently and allowing rollback if needed.

8.6.9 Question: What is a zero-day vulnerability?
Answer: A zero-day vulnerability is a previously unknown security flaw that is exploited by attackers before the software vendor has had a chance to issue a patch.

8.6.10 Question: How do you handle a failed patch deployment?
Answer: Handling a failed patch deployment involves rolling back to the previous stable state, analysing the failure, fixing the issue, and carefully re-deploying the patch.

8.6.11 Question: What is a cumulative patch?

Answer: A cumulative patch is an update that includes multiple previous patches and fixes, allowing systems to be brought up to date with a single installation.

8.6.12 Question: How do you communicate the need for a critical patch to stakeholders?

Answer: Communicate the need for a critical patch by explaining the risks of not applying it, the benefits of the patch, and providing a clear plan for deployment and impact mitigation.

8.6.13 Question: What tools can assist with automated patch management?

Answer: Tools like Microsoft SCCM, WSUS, and third-party solutions like SolarWinds Patch Manager can automate patch deployment, tracking, and reporting.

8.6.14 Question: What is the impact of not applying security patches promptly?

Answer: Not applying security patches promptly can leave systems vulnerable to attacks, resulting in data breaches, compromised systems, and potential legal and financial consequences.

8.6.15 Question: How do you test patches in a production-like environment?

Answer: Test patches in a staging environment that closely mirrors the production setup to identify any issues and ensure compatibility and stability before deployment.

Online Resources

More Practices Questions

Online Exam Paper

URL

https://forms.gle/NMM3gvVY8G9XNK7b7

QR Code

YouTube Video Playlist Link

Chapter 8

URL

https://www.youtube.com/playlist?list=PLzlh_31VWEFp4vzJYBDtKajul4rWTvBur

QR Code

Chapter 9: Planning and Management

9.1 Project Planning and Scheduling

9.1.1 Question: What is project planning?
Answer: Project planning involves defining the project scope, objectives, and steps needed to complete the project, including timelines, resources, and milestones.

9.1.2 Question: Why is project planning important?
Answer: Project planning is crucial for setting clear goals, allocating resources efficiently, managing risks, and ensuring the project stays on track and within budget.

9.1.3 Question: What is a project schedule?
Answer: A project schedule is a timeline that outlines the start and finish dates for project tasks and milestones, helping to manage time and resources effectively.

9.1.4 Question: What are the main components of a project plan?
Answer: The main components include the project scope, objectives, timeline, resource allocation, budget, risk management plan, and stakeholder communication plan.

9.1.5 Question: What is the critical path method (CPM)?
Answer: CPM is a project management technique that identifies the longest sequence of tasks in a project plan, determining the shortest possible project duration.

9.1.6 Question: How do Gantt charts aid in project planning?
Answer: Gantt charts visually represent the project schedule, showing task durations, start and end dates, and dependencies, making it easier to track progress.

9.1.7 Question: What is resource allocation?
Answer: Resource allocation involves assigning available resources, such as people, equipment, and budget, to project tasks to ensure efficient utilization.

9.1.8 Question: What are milestones in project management?
Answer: Milestones are significant points or events in a project timeline that mark the completion of key phases or deliverables, used to measure progress.

9.1.9 Question: What is a Work Breakdown Structure (WBS)?
Answer: A WBS is a hierarchical decomposition of the project into smaller, manageable components or tasks, providing a structured view of what needs to be done.

9.1.10 Question: What is the purpose of a project charter?
Answer: A project charter formally authorizes the project, outlining its objectives, scope, stakeholders, and key roles, providing a clear starting point.

9.1.11 Question: What is risk management in project planning?
Answer: Risk management involves identifying, assessing, and mitigating risks that could impact the project's success, ensuring proactive handling of potential issues.

9.1.12 Question: What is a project baseline?
Answer: A project baseline is the original plan (including scope, schedule, and cost) against which project performance is measured and managed.

9.1.13 Question: What is earned value management (EVM)?
Answer: EVM is a project management technique that combines scope, schedule, and cost data to assess project performance and progress.

9.1.14 Question: How do you handle project scope changes?
Answer: Scope changes are managed through a formal change control process, assessing the impact on time, cost, and resources before approval.

9.1.15 Question: What is a project stakeholder?
Answer: A project stakeholder is any individual or organization that can affect or be affected by the project's outcomes, including sponsors, team members, and end-users.

9.1.16 Question: What is the role of a project manager?
Answer: A project manager is responsible for planning, executing, and closing projects, ensuring they meet objectives, stay on schedule, and remain within budget.

9.1.17 Question: What is project scope management?
Answer: Project scope management involves defining and controlling what is included and excluded in the project, ensuring all required work is completed.

9.1.18 Question: What is a project deliverable?
Answer: A project deliverable is a tangible or intangible output produced as a result of project tasks, such as reports, software, or services.

9.1.19 Question: What is a project kick-off meeting?
Answer: A project kick-off meeting is an initial meeting where stakeholders discuss the project's objectives, scope, roles, and expectations, setting the stage for project execution.

9.1.20 Question: What is a project management plan?
Answer: A project management plan is a comprehensive document that outlines how the project will be executed, monitored, and controlled, including all subsidiary plans.

9.1.21 Question: What is the difference between a project and a program?
Answer: A project is a temporary endeavour with a specific goal and timeline, while a program is a group of related projects managed in a coordinated manner to achieve broader objectives.

9.1.22 Question: What is project scope creep?
Answer: Scope creep refers to uncontrolled changes or continuous growth in a project's scope, often leading to project delays and cost overruns.

9.1.23 Question: What is a project lifecycle?
Answer: A project lifecycle encompasses the stages a project goes through from initiation to closure, typically including initiation, planning, execution, monitoring and control, and closure.

9.1.24 Question: What is a project status report?
Answer: A project status report is a regular update that provides stakeholders with information on project progress, issues, and any changes to the project plan.

9.1.25 Question: How do you prioritize project tasks?
Answer: Project tasks are prioritized based on factors such as urgency, importance, dependencies, and resource availability to ensure critical tasks are completed first.

9.1.26 Question: What is a project dependency?
Answer: A project dependency is a relationship between tasks where one task relies on the completion of another task before it can begin.

9.1.27 Question: What is a project milestone chart?
Answer: A project milestone chart is a graphical representation that highlights key milestones and their dates, helping track significant points in the project timeline.

9.1.28 Question: What is project cost management?
Answer: Project cost management involves estimating, budgeting, and controlling costs to ensure the project can be completed within the approved budget.

9.1.29 Question: What is a risk register?
Answer: A risk register is a document that lists all identified risks, along with their descriptions, probabilities, impacts, and mitigation strategies.

9.1.30 Question: What is project communication management?
Answer: Project communication management involves planning, executing, and monitoring the effective exchange of information among project stakeholders.

9.1.31 Question: What is a project quality plan?
Answer: A project quality plan outlines the quality requirements, standards, and procedures to ensure the project's deliverables meet the expected quality.

9.1.32 Question: What is project scope verification?
Answer: Scope verification is the process of reviewing project deliverables and work results to ensure they meet the defined scope and acceptance criteria.

9.1.33 Question: What is a project post-mortem?
Answer: A project post-mortem is a retrospective analysis conducted after project completion to evaluate what went well, what didn't, and lessons learned.

9.1.34 Question: How do you manage project risks?
Answer: Project risks are managed by identifying, assessing, prioritizing, and developing strategies to mitigate or avoid risks throughout the project lifecycle.

9.1.35 Question: What is the importance of stakeholder engagement?
Answer: Stakeholder engagement is crucial for gaining support, managing expectations, and ensuring that the project meets the needs and interests of all stakeholders.

9.2 Resource Management

9.2.1 Question: What is resource management in project management?
Answer: Resource management involves planning, allocating, and managing the resources required for a project, including human resources, equipment, and materials.

9.2.2 Question: How do you define resource allocation?
Answer: Resource allocation is the process of assigning and managing assets in a manner that supports an organization's strategic goals.

9.2.3 Question: What are the key elements of a resource management plan
Answer: A resource management plan includes resource allocation, resource levelling, utilization, and project scheduling.

9.2.4 Question: What is resource levelling?
Answer: Resource levelling is a technique in project management that resolves resource over-allocations by adjusting the project schedule.

9.2.5 Question: How do you handle resource conflicts in a project?
Answer: Resource conflicts are handled by identifying the conflicts early, communicating with stakeholders, and re-allocating resources or adjusting schedules.

9.2.6 Question: What is a resource breakdown structure (RBS)?
Answer: An RBS is a hierarchical representation of resources by category and type, used to organize and manage project resources.

9.2.7 Question: What is the importance of resource forecasting?
Answer: Resource forecasting predicts future resource requirements to ensure the project has the necessary resources at the right time.

9.2.8 Question: How do you monitor resource utilization?
Answer: Resource utilization is monitored by tracking resource usage against the project plan and making adjustments as necessary.

9.2.9 Question: What are some common tools used for resource management?
Answer: Common tools include Gantt charts, resource histograms, project management software like MS Project, and resource tracking spreadsheets.

9.2.10 Question: How does resource management impact project success?
Answer: Effective resource management ensures that the right resources are available at the right time, leading to timely project completion and optimal use of resources.

9.2.11 Question: What is a resource calendar?
Answer: A resource calendar is a calendar that specifies when project resources are available or allocated for project work.

9.2.12 Question: Why is it important to have a balanced workload for resources?
Answer: A balanced workload prevents burnout, maintains productivity, and ensures that resources are effectively utilized throughout the project.

9.2.13 Question: How can you optimize resource allocation?
Answer: Resource allocation can be optimized by prioritizing tasks, reallocating resources based on availability and skills, and using resource management tools.

9.2.14 Question: What is the role of communication in resource management?
Answer: Communication ensures that all stakeholders are aware of resource needs, availability, and allocation, facilitating better coordination and problem resolution.

9.2.15 Question: How do you handle resource shortages in a project?
Answer: Resource shortages can be handled by reallocating existing resources, hiring additional resources, outsourcing, or rescheduling project tasks.

9.2.16 Question: What is the significance of resource dependencies?
Answer: Resource dependencies highlight the relationships between tasks and resources, helping in planning and managing resource allocation effectively.

9.2.17 Question: What are the challenges in resource management?
Answer: Challenges include resource conflicts, overallocation, shortages, underutilization, and maintaining resource productivity.

9.2.18 Question: How do you measure resource performance?
Answer: Resource performance is measured by tracking metrics such as utilization rate, efficiency, productivity, and adherence to the project schedule.

9.2.19 Question: What strategies can you use for effective resource management?
Answer: Strategies include detailed planning, regular monitoring, using management tools, efficient communication, and flexibility in resource allocation.

9.2.20 Question: What is a resource pool?
Answer: A resource pool is a collection of resources available for allocation to project tasks, including personnel, equipment, and materials.

9.2.21 Question: How does resource availability affect project scheduling?
Answer: Resource availability directly impacts project scheduling as tasks can only be assigned and completed if the necessary resources are available.

9.2.22 Question: What is resource smoothing?
Answer: Resource smoothing is a technique that adjusts activities within their float to achieve a uniform distribution of resource usage.

9.2.23 Question: Why is it important to track resource costs?
Answer: Tracking resource costs is important to ensure the project stays within budget and to make informed decisions about resource allocation.

9.2.24 Question: How do you manage resource risks?
Answer: Resource risks are managed by identifying potential risks early, creating contingency plans, and continuously monitoring and adjusting resource plans.

9.2.25 Question: What is the difference between resource levelling and resource smoothing?
Answer: Resource levelling adjusts the project schedule to resolve resource conflicts, while resource smoothing aims to evenly distribute resource usage without affecting the critical path.

9.2.26 Question: How do you handle resource overallocation?
Answer: Resource overallocation can be handled by extending deadlines, hiring additional resources, or reallocating tasks among available resources.

9.2.27 Question: What is the role of a resource manager?
Answer: A resource manager is responsible for planning, allocating, and managing resources to ensure efficient project execution.

9.2.28 Question: How can technology aid in resource management?
Answer: Technology aids resource management by providing tools for planning, tracking, and analysing resource usage, improving efficiency and decision-making.

9.2.29 Question: What is a resource allocation matrix?
Answer: A resource allocation matrix is a tool used to map resources to specific tasks, providing a visual representation of resource assignments.

9.2.30 Question: How do you ensure resource efficiency in a project?
Answer: Resource efficiency is ensured by optimizing resource allocation, avoiding overallocation, using management tools, and regularly monitoring resource performance.

9.2.31 Question: What are resource constraints?
Answer: Resource constraints are limitations on the availability and capacity of resources, impacting project scheduling and execution.

9.2.32 Question: How do you balance resource utilization and project deadlines?
Answer: Balancing resource utilization and project deadlines requires careful planning, continuous monitoring, and adjusting resource allocation and schedules as needed.

9.2.33 Question: What is the importance of resource planning in project management?
Answer: Resource planning is crucial for ensuring that the right resources are available at the right time, preventing delays, and optimizing resource use.

9.2.34 Question: How do you handle changes in resource availability?
Answer: Changes in resource availability are handled by reassessing the resource plan, communicating with stakeholders, and adjusting schedules or reallocating tasks as necessary.

9.2.35 Question: What is the impact of poor resource management on a project?
Answer: Poor resource management can lead to project delays, increased costs, resource conflicts, and reduced project quality.

9.3 Risk Management

9.3.1 Question: What is risk management in project management?
Answer: Risk management involves identifying, assessing, and prioritizing risks followed by coordinating resources to minimize, monitor, and control the probability and impact of unforeseen events.

9.3.2 Question: How do you identify project risks?
Answer: Project risks are identified through techniques such as brainstorming, SWOT analysis, expert judgment, and reviewing project documentation and lessons learned.

9.3.3 Question: What is a risk register?
Answer: A risk register is a document that lists all identified risks, their severity, and the actions steps to manage them, serving as a central repository for risk information.

9.3.4 Question: What are the steps in the risk management process?
Answer: The steps include risk identification, risk assessment, risk prioritization, risk response planning, and risk monitoring and control.

9.3.5 Question: What is qualitative risk analysis?
Answer: Qualitative risk analysis assesses the impact and likelihood of identified risks using subjective judgment to prioritize them for further action.

9.3.6 Question: What is quantitative risk analysis?
Answer: Quantitative risk analysis uses numerical methods and statistical techniques to evaluate the impact of risks on project objectives.

9.3.7 Question: How do you prioritize risks?
Answer: Risks are prioritized based on their potential impact on the project and the likelihood of their occurrence using risk matrices or scoring systems.

9.3.8 Question: What is a risk response strategy?
Answer: A risk response strategy involves developing options and actions to enhance opportunities and reduce threats to project objectives, such as avoidance, mitigation, transfer, or acceptance.

9.3.9 Question: What is risk mitigation?
Answer: Risk mitigation involves taking proactive steps to reduce the likelihood or impact of a risk event.

9.3.10 Question: What is risk avoidance?
Answer: Risk avoidance involves changing the project plan to eliminate the risk or protect project objectives from its impact.

9.3.11 Question: What is risk transfer?
Answer: Risk transfer involves shifting the impact of a risk to a third party, such as through insurance or outsourcing.

9.3.12 Question: What is risk acceptance?
Answer: Risk acceptance acknowledges the risk and decides to take no action unless the risk occurs, suitable for low-impact or low-probability risks.

9.3.13 Question: What is a contingency plan?

Answer: A contingency plan is a predefined set of actions to be taken if a risk event occurs, designed to mitigate its impact on the project.

9.3.14 Question: How do you monitor and control project risks?
Answer: Project risks are monitored and controlled through regular risk reviews, risk audits, and tracking risk indicators to ensure timely response.

9.3.15 Question: What is a risk owner?
Answer: A risk owner is a person responsible for managing a specific risk, including developing and implementing risk response strategies.

9.3.16 Question: How do you communicate risks to stakeholders?
Answer: Risks are communicated to stakeholders through regular project meetings, risk reports, and updates to the risk register, ensuring transparency and involvement.

9.3.17 Question: What is residual risk?
Answer: Residual risk is the remaining risk after risk responses have been implemented, often requiring monitoring and additional action if necessary.

9.3.18 Question: What is secondary risk?
Answer: Secondary risk is a new risk that arises as a direct result of implementing a risk response strategy.

9.3.19 Question: What is a risk threshold?
Answer: A risk threshold is the level of risk exposure above which risks are deemed unacceptable and below which risks are accepted without further action.

9.3.20 Question: What is a risk appetite?
Answer: Risk appetite is the amount and type of risk that an organization is willing to take in order to meet its objectives.

9.3.21 Question: What is the difference between risk management and issue management?
Answer: Risk management deals with potential future events that may impact the project, while issue management addresses current problems that are affecting the project.

9.3.22 Question: How do you use a risk matrix?
Answer: A risk matrix is used to assess and prioritize risks by mapping the likelihood of occurrence against the impact on project objectives.

9.3.23 Question: What is the importance of risk management in system analysis and design?
Answer: Risk management is crucial in system analysis and design to identify potential issues early, ensure project stability, and meet project objectives efficiently.

9.3.24 Question: How do you integrate risk management into project planning?
Answer: Risk management is integrated into project planning by identifying risks during the planning phase and developing appropriate response strategies as part of the project plan.

9.3.25 Question: What is the role of a risk manager?
Answer: A risk manager is responsible for overseeing the risk management process, including identifying risks, assessing their impact, and developing risk response strategies.

9.3.26 Question: How do you handle unknown risks in a project?
Answer: Unknown risks are handled by maintaining contingency reserves and creating a flexible project plan that can adapt to unexpected events.

9.3.27 Question: What are the common risk management tools and techniques?

Answer: Common tools and techniques include risk registers, risk matrices, SWOT analysis, Monte Carlo simulation, and decision trees.

9.3.28 Question: What is risk tolerance?
Answer: Risk tolerance is the degree of variability in project outcomes that stakeholders are willing to accept.

9.3.29 Question: How do you assess the impact of a risk?
Answer: The impact of a risk is assessed by evaluating its potential effect on project objectives, including cost, schedule, quality, and scope.

9.3.30 Question: What is a risk management plan?
Answer: A risk management plan outlines the approach, resources, and activities for managing project risks, including roles, responsibilities, and risk response strategies.

9.3.31 Question: How do you ensure continuous risk management throughout a project?
Answer: Continuous risk management is ensured through regular risk assessments, updates to the risk register, and ongoing communication with the project team and stakeholders.

9.3.32 Question: What is the importance of risk documentation?
Answer: Risk documentation is important for tracking identified risks, their assessments, and responses, providing a reference for decision-making and lessons learned.

9.3.33 Question: How do you evaluate the effectiveness of risk responses?
Answer: The effectiveness of risk responses is evaluated by monitoring the impact of the response on the risk and project objectives and adjusting as necessary.

9.3.34 Question: What is risk probability?
Answer: Risk probability is the likelihood that a risk event will occur, often expressed as a percentage or on a scale from low to high.

9.3.35 Question: How does organizational culture influence risk management?
Answer: Organizational culture influences risk management by shaping attitudes towards risk-taking, risk communication, and the level of rigor applied to the risk management process.

9.4 Project Communication

9.4.1 Question: What is project communication management?
Answer: Project communication management involves planning, executing, and monitoring the communication strategies to ensure effective information flow among project stakeholders.

9.4.2 Question: Why is effective communication important in a project?
Answer: Effective communication ensures that all stakeholders are informed, aligned, and engaged, which is crucial for project success and smooth execution.

9.4.3 Question: What are the key components of a project communication plan?
Answer: Key components include communication objectives, target audience, message content, communication methods, frequency, and responsible parties.

9.4.4 Question: How do you determine the communication needs of a project?
Answer: Communication needs are determined by analysing stakeholder requirements, project complexity, and the type of information that needs to be shared.

9.4.5 Question: What are some common communication methods used in projects?
Answer: Common methods include meetings, emails, reports, dashboards, and collaboration tools like Slack or Microsoft Teams.

9.4.6 Question: What is the role of a project manager in communication management?
Answer: The project manager is responsible for ensuring effective communication among stakeholders, facilitating meetings, and resolving any communication issues.

9.4.7 Question: How do you handle communication barriers in a project?
Answer: Communication barriers are handled by identifying the causes, using clear and concise language, ensuring proper channels, and encouraging feedback.

9.4.8 Question: What is the importance of stakeholder communication?
Answer: Stakeholder communication is crucial for gaining support, managing expectations, and ensuring that project objectives align with stakeholder needs.

9.4.9 Question: How do you ensure that all stakeholders are informed about project progress?
Answer: Regular updates, status reports, meetings, and dashboards are used to keep stakeholders informed about project progress and any issues.

9.4.10 Question: What is a communication matrix?
Answer: A communication matrix is a tool that outlines the communication plan, specifying what information will be shared, with whom, how, and when.

9.4.11 Question: How do you manage communication in a geographically dispersed team?
Answer: Communication in dispersed teams is managed through virtual meetings, collaboration tools, time zone considerations, and clear communication protocols.

9.4.12 Question: What is the role of feedback in project communication?
Answer: Feedback ensures that the communication is effective, helps identify any issues, and allows for adjustments to improve the communication process.

9.4.13 Question: How do you use technology to enhance project communication?
Answer: Technology enhances communication through project management tools, collaboration platforms, instant messaging, video conferencing, and shared documents.

9.4.14 Question: What is the importance of documenting project communications?
Answer: Documentation provides a record of communications, decisions, and actions, ensuring transparency and accountability throughout the project.

9.4.15 Question: How do you communicate project risks to stakeholders?
Answer: Project risks are communicated through risk reports, meetings, and updates that outline the risks, their impact, and mitigation strategies.

9.4.16 Question: What is a communication audit?
Answer: A communication audit is a review of the project's communication processes to evaluate their effectiveness and identify areas for improvement.

9.4.17 Question: How do you tailor communication to different stakeholder groups?
Answer: Communication is tailored by understanding each group's needs, preferences, and the level of detail required, and using appropriate methods and language.

9.4.18 Question: What is the impact of poor communication on a project?
Answer: Poor communication can lead to misunderstandings, missed deadlines, stakeholder dissatisfaction, and ultimately project failure.

9.4.19 Question: How do you ensure clarity and conciseness in project communication?
Answer: Clarity and conciseness are ensured by using simple language, avoiding jargon, being specific, and focusing on key messages.

9.4.20 Question: How do you handle sensitive information in project communication?
Answer: Sensitive information is handled by limiting access to authorized personnel, using secure channels, and clearly marking confidential information.

9.4.21 Question: What is the significance of a project kick-off meeting?
Answer: A kick-off meeting sets the stage for the project, establishes communication channels, clarifies roles, and aligns the team on objectives and expectations.

9.4.22 Question: How do you manage communication during a project crisis?
Answer: During a crisis, clear, timely, and transparent communication is crucial, focusing on the issue, impact, resolution steps, and keeping stakeholders informed.

9.4.23 Question: What are some best practices for effective project communication?
Answer: Best practices include regular updates, active listening, clear messaging, using appropriate tools, and encouraging open dialogue.

9.4.24 Question: How do you measure the effectiveness of project communication?
Answer: Effectiveness is measured through stakeholder feedback, communication audits, and evaluating if communication objectives are being met.

9.4.25 Question: How do you handle conflicting communication styles within a team?
Answer: Conflicting styles are handled by promoting understanding, adapting communication approaches, facilitating mediation, and establishing common ground.

Online Resources

More Practices Questions

Online Exam Paper

URL

https://forms.gle/1dfvQwgED7F7iNvW9

QR Code

YouTube Video Playlist Link

Chapter 9

URL

https://www.youtube.com/playlist?list=PLzlh_31VWEFrHxX2YTfTF6TYNTnr-CxJm

QR Code

Chapter 10: Quality Assurance

10.1 Testing Fundamentals

10.1.1 Question: What is software testing?
Answer: Software testing is the process of evaluating and verifying that a software application or system meets specified requirements and functions correctly.

10.1.2 Question: What are the main objectives of software testing?
Answer: The main objectives are to identify defects, ensure the software meets requirements, and validate that the system performs as expected in different scenarios.

10.1.3 Question: What is the difference between verification and validation?
Answer: Verification ensures the product is built correctly according to specifications, while validation checks if the right product is built, **meeting** user needs.

10.1.4 Question: What are the different levels of testing?
Answer: The levels include unit testing, integration testing, system testing, and acceptance testing, each focusing on different aspects of the system.

10.1.5 Question: What is unit testing?
Answer: Unit testing involves testing individual components or modules of a software application to ensure they function correctly in **isolation**.

10.1.6 Question: What is integration testing?
Answer: Integration testing evaluates the interaction between integrated modules to detect interface defects and ensure they work together as **intended**.

10.1.7 Question: What is system testing?
Answer: System **testing** verifies that the complete and integrated software system meets the specified requirements and performs correctly.

10.1.8 Question: What is acceptance testing?
Answer: Acceptance testing is conducted to determine whether the system meets the acceptance criteria and is ready for deployment, often performed by end-users.

10.1.9 Question: What is regression testing?
Answer: Regression testing ensures that new code changes do not adversely affect existing functionality of the software system.

10.1.10 Question: What is a test case?
Answer: A test case is a set of conditions or variables under which a tester determines whether a software system is working correctly.

10.1.11 Question: What is a test plan?
Answer: A test plan is a document detailing the objectives, resources, schedule, and scope of testing activities, guiding the testing process.

10.1.12 Question: What is test coverage?
Answer: Test coverage measures the extent to which the source code is tested by the test suite, ensuring all parts of the code are examined.

10.1.13 Question: What is the purpose of a test environment?
Answer: A test **environment** provides the setup for testing, including hardware, software, network configurations, and necessary tools to simulate the production environment.

10.1.14 Question: What is automated testing?
Answer: Automated testing uses software tools to execute tests automatically, compare actual outcomes with expected outcomes, and report **results**.

10.1.15 Question: What are the benefits of automated testing?
Answer: Benefits include increased test coverage, faster execution, repeatability, and the ability to run tests unattended, improving efficiency and accuracy.

10.1.16 Question: What is manual testing?
Answer: Manual testing involves human testers executing test cases without the use of automation tools, relying on their observations to identify defects.

10.1.17 Question: What is black-box testing?
Answer: Black-box testing evaluates the software's functionality without examining the internal code structure, focusing on inputs and outputs.

10.1.18 Question: What is white-box testing?
Answer: White-box testing involves testing the internal structures or workings of an application, requiring knowledge of the source code.

10.1.19 Question: What is performance testing?
Answer: Performance testing assesses the speed, responsiveness, and stability of a software application under a particular workload.

10.1.20 Question: What is load testing?
Answer: Load testing evaluates how a system behaves under a specific load, identifying the maximum operating capacity and any bottlenecks.

10.1.21 Question: What is stress testing?
Answer: Stress testing involves testing the system under extreme conditions to determine its breaking point and how it recovers from failure.

10.1.22 Question: What is usability testing?
Answer: Usability testing assesses how easy and user-friendly a software application is by observing real users as they interact with the system.

10.1.23 Question: What is security testing?
Answer: Security testing identifies vulnerabilities, threats, and risks in a software application to ensure data protection and maintain functionality.

10.1.24 Question: What is alpha testing?
Answer: Alpha testing is an internal testing phase conducted by developers and testers within the organization to identify bugs before releasing the software to external users.

10.1.25 Question: What is beta testing?
Answer: Beta testing involves releasing the software to a limited number of external users to gain feedback and identify issues before the final release.

10.1.26 Question: What is test automation framework?
Answer: A test automation framework is a set of guidelines, standards, and tools for creating and managing automated test scripts efficiently.

10.1.27 Question: What is defect life cycle?
Answer: The defect life cycle describes the stages a defect goes through from identification to resolution, including new, assigned, fixed, retested, and closed.

10.1.28 Question: What is exploratory testing?
Answer: Exploratory testing involves simultaneously learning about the system, designing tests, and executing them to discover defects not covered by predefined test cases.

10.1.29 Question: What is a test script?
Answer: A test script is a set of instructions executed by an automated testing tool to perform a specific test on the software application.

10.1.30 Question: What is test data?
Answer: Test data is the data used by test cases to test a software application's functionality and performance, including valid, invalid, and boundary data.

10.1.31 Question: What is defect triage?
Answer: Defect triage is the process of reviewing, prioritizing, and assigning defects to ensure critical issues are addressed promptly.

10.1.32 Question: What is static testing?
Answer: Static testing involves reviewing and analysing the software's documentation, code, and requirements without executing the code.

10.1.33 Question: What is dynamic testing?
Answer: Dynamic testing involves executing the software code to validate its functionality and performance against specified requirements.

10.1.34 Question: What is end-to-end testing?
Answer: End-to-end testing validates the complete workflow of a system, ensuring all integrated components function together as expected.

10.1.35 Question: What is a smoke test?
Answer: A smoke test is a preliminary test to check the basic functionality of the software, ensuring it is stable enough for further testing.

10.2 Test Planning and Strategy

10.2.1 Question: What is test planning?
Answer: Test planning is the process of defining the scope, approach, resources, and schedule of testing activities to ensure that the system meets its requirements and performs as expected.

10.2.2 Question: Why is a test strategy important?
Answer: A test strategy outlines the testing approach and ensures consistency, efficiency, and effectiveness in identifying defects and verifying system functionality.

10.2.3 Question: What are the key components of a test plan?
Answer: Key components include test objectives, scope, resources, schedule, test environment, test deliverables, and risk assessment.

10.2.4 Question: What is the difference between test planning and test strategy?
Answer: Test planning is a detailed, project-specific document outlining how testing will be conducted, while a test strategy is a high-level document that defines the overall approach and guidelines for testing.

10.2.5 Question: What is risk-based testing?
Answer: Risk-based testing prioritizes testing activities based on the risk of failure and its impact, ensuring that the most critical parts of the system are tested first.

10.2.6 Question: What is a test case?

Answer: A test case is a set of conditions or variables used to determine whether a system or component is working correctly.

10.2.7 Question: What is a test scenario?
Answer: A test scenario is a high-level description of a functionality to be tested, which includes multiple test cases to validate that functionality.

10.2.8 Question: What is a test suite?
Answer: A test suite is a collection of test cases that are intended to be executed together to test a particular feature or functionality.

10.2.9 Question: What is regression testing?
Answer: Regression testing involves re-running previously conducted tests after changes are made to ensure that new code changes do not adversely affect existing functionality.

10.2.10 Question: What is the purpose of a test environment?
Answer: A test environment replicates the production environment to the extent possible, providing a controlled setting where tests can be executed to ensure reliability and consistency.

10.2.11 Question: What is test automation?
Answer: Test automation uses software tools to execute pre-scripted tests on a software application before it is released into production, enhancing efficiency and coverage.

10.2.12 Question: What are the benefits of automated testing?
Answer: Benefits include faster execution, increased test coverage, repeatability, consistency, and the ability to run tests unattended.

10.2.13 Question: What is a test script?
Answer: A test script is a set of instructions executed by automated testing tools to perform a specific test on the application.

10.2.14 Question: What is the role of a test manager?
Answer: A test manager oversees the testing activities, ensures resources are properly allocated, manages the test team, and communicates the status and results of testing to stakeholders.

10.2.15 Question: What is the difference between white-box testing and black-box testing?
Answer: White-box testing involves testing the internal structures or workings of an application, while black-box testing focuses on testing the functionality without knowing the internal code.

10.2.16 Question: What is performance testing?
Answer: Performance testing evaluates how a system performs under various conditions, such as load, stress, and scalability, to ensure it meets performance requirements.

10.2.17 Question: What is load testing?
Answer: Load testing measures how a system behaves under an expected load of concurrent users or transactions to ensure it can handle high usage.

10.2.18 Question: What is stress testing?
Answer: Stress testing involves testing a system beyond its normal operational capacity to determine its breaking point and how it recovers from failure.

10.2.19 Question: What is user acceptance testing (UAT)?
Answer: UAT is performed by the end-users to ensure the system meets their requirements and is ready for production use.

10.2.20 Question: What is a test coverage metric?

Answer: Test coverage metrics quantify the extent to which the test cases cover the requirements or code, helping to identify untested parts of the application.

10.2.21 Question: What is exploratory testing?
Answer: Exploratory testing is an informal, unscripted testing approach where testers explore the application to identify defects based on their intuition and experience.

10.2.22 Question: What is a defect life cycle?
Answer: The defect life cycle, or bug life cycle, describes the various stages a defect goes through from identification to resolution and closure.

10.2.23 Question: What is the role of a QA analyst?
Answer: A QA analyst is responsible for designing, implementing, and executing test plans and cases to ensure the software meets the required quality standards.

10.2.24 Question: What is the purpose of a test summary report?
Answer: A test summary report provides an overview of the testing activities, including the number of tests executed, defects found, and the overall quality of the system.

10.2.25 Question: What is continuous integration testing?
Answer: Continuous integration testing involves automatically testing the application every time new code is integrated, ensuring early detection of defects.

10.2.26 Question: What is the difference between alpha testing and beta testing?
Answer: Alpha testing is performed by internal testers before the software is released to external users, while beta testing is conducted by actual users in a real-world environment before the final release.

10.2.27 Question: What is the V-Model in software testing?
Answer: The V-Model, or Verification and Validation model, is a software development model that emphasizes parallel testing activities with corresponding development stages.

10.2.28 Question: What is the role of a test data?
Answer: Test data is the data used in test cases to simulate real-world scenarios and validate the functionality of the system.

10.2.29 Question: What is smoke testing?
Answer: Smoke testing is a preliminary test to check the basic functionality of an application before conducting more detailed testing.

10.2.30 Question: What is sanity testing?
Answer: Sanity testing is a subset of regression testing focused on verifying specific functionalities after minor changes to ensure they work as expected.

10.2.31 Question: What is boundary value analysis?
Answer: Boundary value analysis is a testing technique that involves creating test cases that focus on the boundary values of input domains to identify potential defects.

10.2.32 Question: What is equivalence partitioning?
Answer: Equivalence partitioning is a testing technique that divides input data into equivalent partitions, where test cases from each partition are expected to uncover similar defects.

10.2.33 Question: What is a test execution schedule?
Answer: A test execution schedule outlines the timeline and sequence in which test cases will be executed during the testing phase.

10.2.34 Question: What is defect triage?

Answer: Defect triage is the process of prioritizing and assigning defects based on their severity, impact, and urgency to ensure the most critical issues are addressed first.

10.2.35 Question: What is a test closure activity?
Answer: Test closure activities involve finalizing and documenting the testing process, including test results, defect logs, and lessons learned, ensuring all testing objectives have been met

10.3 Types of Testing

10.3.1 Question: What is unit testing?
Answer: Unit testing involves testing individual components or modules of a system to ensure they function correctly. It is typically performed by developers during the coding phase.

10.3.2 Question: What is integration testing?
Answer: Integration testing verifies the interactions between integrated units or components to detect interface defects. It ensures that combined modules work together as expected.

10.3.3 Question: What is system testing?
Answer: System testing evaluates the complete and integrated system to verify that it meets the specified requirements. It checks the system's overall functionality, performance, and reliability.

10.3.4 Question: What is acceptance testing?
Answer: Acceptance testing is conducted to determine whether a system meets the business requirements and is ready for deployment. It is often performed by end-users or clients.

10.3.5 Question: What is regression testing?
Answer: Regression testing involves retesting a system after changes or updates to ensure that existing functionalities still work correctly and that new defects have not been introduced.

10.3.6 Question: What is performance testing?
Answer: Performance testing assesses the system's responsiveness, stability, and scalability under various load conditions. It includes load testing, stress testing, and endurance testing.

10.3.7 Question: What is load testing?
Answer: Load testing evaluates the system's performance under expected user load conditions. It helps identify performance bottlenecks and ensures the system can handle anticipated traffic.

10.3.8 Question: What is stress testing?
Answer: Stress testing involves testing the system beyond its normal operational capacity to determine its robustness and identify the breaking point under extreme conditions.

10.3.9 Question: What is usability testing?
Answer: Usability testing assesses how easily and effectively end-users can interact with the system. It focuses on the user experience, including the interface design and overall usability.

10.3.10 Question: What is security testing?
Answer: Security testing evaluates the system's ability to protect data and maintain functionality despite malicious attacks. It includes testing for vulnerabilities, encryption, and access controls.

10.3.11 Question: What is compatibility testing?
Answer: Compatibility testing ensures that the system works correctly across different browsers, devices, operating systems, and network environments.

10.3.12 Question: What is alpha testing?
Answer: Alpha testing is an initial testing phase conducted by internal staff or developers to identify and fix bugs before the software is released to external testers or customers.

10.3.13 Question: What is beta testing?
Answer: Beta testing is performed by actual users in a real-world environment to provide feedback on the software's performance, usability, and reliability before the final release.

10.3.14 Question: What is exploratory testing?
Answer: Exploratory testing involves simultaneous learning, test design, and execution by testers who actively explore the system without predefined test cases.

10.3.15 Question: What is automated testing?
Answer: Automated testing uses scripts and tools to execute test cases automatically, reducing manual effort and increasing testing efficiency and coverage.

10.3.16 Question: What is manual testing?
Answer: Manual testing requires testers to execute test cases manually without automation tools, focusing on flexibility and adaptability to unexpected issues.

10.3.17 Question: What is functional testing?
Answer: Functional testing validates that the system's functionalities work according to specified requirements, ensuring that all features perform as expected.

10.3.18 Question: What is non-functional testing?
Answer: Non-functional testing evaluates aspects such as performance, usability, reliability, and security, focusing on how the system operates rather than specific behaviours.

10.3.19 Question: What is white-box testing?
Answer: White-box testing involves testing the internal structures or workings of an application, requiring knowledge of the code and often used to test specific paths or conditions.

10.3.20 Question: What is black-box testing?
Answer: Black-box testing assesses the system's functionality without knowledge of its internal code or structure, focusing on input-output behaviour.

10.3.21 Question: What is gray-box testing?
Answer: Gray-box testing combines aspects of both white-box and black-box testing, using limited knowledge of the internal workings to design effective test cases.

10.3.22 Question: What is smoke testing?
Answer: Smoke testing is a preliminary test to check the basic functionality of a system, ensuring that the most critical features work and the system is stable enough for further testing.

10.3.23 Question: What is sanity testing?
Answer: Sanity testing is a subset of regression testing focused on verifying that specific functionalities work correctly after minor changes or bug fixes.

10.3.24 Question: What is end-to-end testing?
Answer: End-to-end testing validates the entire application flow, from start to finish, to ensure that all components and integrations work together as expected.

10.3.25 Question: What is user acceptance testing (UAT)?
Answer: UAT is performed by the end-users to verify that the system meets their needs and requirements, serving as the final validation before production deployment.

10.3.26 Question: What is interface testing?
Answer: Interface testing checks the interactions between different system components or systems, ensuring they communicate and function together correctly.

10.3.27 Question: What is installation testing?

Answer: Installation testing verifies that the software installs correctly in the target environment and that it functions as expected post-installation.

10.3.28 Question: What is recovery testing?

Answer: Recovery testing assesses the system's ability to recover from crashes, hardware failures, or other catastrophic issues, ensuring data integrity and system stability.

10.3.29 Question: What is maintenance testing?

Answer: Maintenance testing involves testing modifications or updates made to an existing system to ensure they do not introduce new defects and that the system continues to function correctly.

10.3.30 Question: What is localization testing?

Answer: Localization testing ensures that the software adapts correctly to different languages, regional settings, and cultural contexts, providing a suitable user experience globally.

10.3.31 Question: What is internationalization testing?

Answer: Internationalization testing verifies that the software can be easily adapted for various languages and regions without requiring significant changes to the codebase.

10.3.32 Question: What is ad-hoc testing?

Answer: Ad-hoc testing is an informal testing approach where testers try to break the system without any specific plan or documentation, relying on intuition and experience.

10.3.33 Question: What is dynamic testing?

Answer: Dynamic testing involves executing the code and validating the system's behaviour during runtime, including functional and non-functional testing types.

10.3.34 Question: What is static testing?

Answer: Static testing involves reviewing the code, requirements, or design documents without executing the code, aiming to identify errors early in the development process.

10.3.35 Question: What is mutation testing?

Answer: Mutation testing involves introducing small changes to the program's code to check if existing test cases can detect the changes, assessing the quality of the test cases.

10.4 Test Automation

10.4.1 Question: What is test automation?

Answer: Test automation involves using specialized software tools to execute tests automatically, manage test data, and analyse results, improving efficiency and accuracy in the testing process.

10.4.2 Question: What are the benefits of test automation?

Answer: Test automation improves test coverage, increases test execution speed, reduces manual effort, enhances accuracy, and enables frequent regression testing.

10.4.3 Question: What types of tests can be automated?

Answer: Common tests that can be automated include unit tests, integration tests, functional tests, regression tests, and performance tests.

10.4.4 Question: What is a test automation framework?

Answer: A test automation framework provides a structured approach to automated testing, including guidelines, tools, and practices to create and execute test scripts efficiently.

10.4.5 Question: Can you name some popular test automation tools?

Answer: Popular test automation tools include Selenium, QTP/UFT, TestComplete, Appium, and JUnit.

10.4.6 Question: What is Selenium?
Answer: Selenium is an open-source test automation tool for web applications, supporting multiple programming languages and browsers.

10.4.7 Question: What is the role of a test automation engineer?
Answer: A test automation engineer designs, develops, and maintains automated test scripts, ensuring the efficiency and reliability of the test automation process.

10.4.8 Question: What is a regression test in the context of automation?
Answer: Regression tests verify that new changes have not adversely affected existing functionality, ensuring the software remains stable after updates.

10.4.9 Question: What is a test script?
Answer: A test script is a set of instructions written in a programming or scripting language to perform automated testing tasks.

10.4.10 Question: What are the challenges of test automation?
Answer: Challenges include high initial setup costs, maintaining test scripts with changing requirements, selecting the right tools, and managing test data.

10.4.11 Question: How do you decide which tests to automate?
Answer: Tests that are repetitive, time-consuming, and require frequent execution are good candidates for automation. Critical business workflows and high-risk areas should also be considered.

10.4.12 Question: What is continuous integration (CI) in test automation?
Answer: Continuous integration involves automatically running tests every time code is committed to the repository, ensuring that changes integrate smoothly with the existing codebase.

10.4.13 Question: What is the role of version control in test automation?
Answer: Version control systems track changes to test scripts and test data, enabling collaboration among team members and maintaining a history of modifications.

10.4.14 Question: What is data-driven testing?
Answer: Data-driven testing involves executing test scripts with multiple sets of data inputs to validate that the application behaves as expected under different conditions.

10.4.15 Question: What is keyword-driven testing?
Answer: Keyword-driven testing uses a set of predefined keywords to represent actions in test scripts, making it easier to write and understand tests without deep programming knowledge.

10.4.16 Question: How do you handle dynamic elements in automated testing?
Answer: Handling dynamic elements involves using strategies like XPath with dynamic attributes, waiting mechanisms, and maintaining a locator strategy to identify elements reliably.

10.4.17 Question: What is test coverage in automation?
Answer: Test coverage measures the extent to which the automated tests cover the application's code, functionalities, and requirements.

10.4.18 Question: What is the Page Object Model (POM)?
Answer: POM is a design pattern in test automation that creates an object repository for web elements, promoting code reuse and maintainability.

10.4.19 Question: What is a smoke test in test automation?

Answer: A smoke test is a quick, initial test to check the basic functionality of an application, ensuring that critical features work before more detailed testing.

10.4.20 Question: What is a test suite?
Answer: A test suite is a collection of test cases or scripts designed to validate a specific aspect of an application or the entire application.

10.4.21 Question: How do you measure the success of test automation?
Answer: Success can be measured by metrics such as test execution speed, defect detection rate, test coverage, and reduction in manual testing effort.

10.4.22 Question: What is the difference between scripless and script-based test automation?
Answer: Scripless test automation uses visual interfaces and predefined actions to create tests without coding, while script-based automation involves writing test scripts in a programming language.

10.4.23 Question: What is cross-browser testing in automation?
Answer: Cross-browser testing ensures that web applications function correctly across different web browsers, validating compatibility and user experience.

10.4.24 Question: How do you handle test data in automation?
Answer: Test data can be managed using techniques like data parameterization, external data sources (e.g., databases, CSV files), and data-driven frameworks.

10.4.25 Question: What is the role of logging in test automation?
Answer: Logging captures detailed information about test execution, including errors and test results, aiding in debugging and analysing test failures.

10.4.26 Question: What is headless browser testing?
Answer: Headless browser testing involves running browser tests without a graphical user interface, improving test execution speed and resource usage.

10.4.27 Question: How do you ensure maintainability in test automation?
Answer: Maintainability is ensured by following best practices like modular test design, using reusable components, maintaining a robust locator strategy, and regular refactoring.

10.4.28 Question: What is a test management tool?
Answer: A test management tool helps plan, execute, and track testing activities, managing test cases, test scripts, defects, and reporting metrics.

10.4.29 Question: How does automated testing integrate with DevOps?
Answer: Automated testing integrates with DevOps by incorporating continuous testing in the CI/CD pipeline, enabling rapid feedback and facilitating continuous delivery.

10.4.30 Question: What is behaviour-**driven development (BDD) in test automation?**
Answer: BDD is a software development approach where tests are written in a natural language that non-technical stakeholders can understand, fostering collaboration and ensuring requirements are met.

10.4.31 Question: What is the importance of test automation in Agile methodology?
Answer: Test automation in Agile ensures that frequent iterations and continuous integration are supported by automated tests, maintaining code quality and reducing manual effort.

10.4.32 Question: How do you deal with flaky tests in automation?
Answer: Flaky tests, which produce inconsistent results, can be managed by improving test stability, enhancing wait conditions, and isolating and fixing underlying issues.

10.4.33 Question: What is a hybrid test automation framework?

Answer: A hybrid test automation framework combines the features of different frameworks, such as data-driven, keyword-driven, and modular frameworks, to leverage their strengths.

10.4.34 Question: What is a CI/CD pipeline?
Answer: A CI/CD pipeline automates the process of integrating code changes, running tests, and deploying applications, ensuring rapid and reliable software delivery.

10.4.35 Question: What are the best practices for writing test scripts?
Answer: Best practices include keeping scripts simple and modular, using clear and descriptive names, implementing robust error handling, and maintaining up-to-date documentation.

Online Resources

More Practices Questions

Online Exam Paper

URL

https://forms.gle/Na32uYgmXk1NgqRYA

QR Code

YouTube Video Playlist Link

Chapter 10

URL

https://www.youtube.com/playlist?list=PLzlh_31VWEFrJ-VsasUrJ2Ts0HAwUnmfX

QR Code

ADDITIONAL RESOURCES

System analysis and design Interview Questions & Answers Videos Playlist-

Link: https://www.youtube.com/playlist?list=PLzlh_31VWEFpoXqf9ap0Pw8Rs-sf8fgyx

QR Code:

YouTube Videos Playlists for all Chapters

CHAPTER 1
Link: https://www.youtube.com/playlist?list=PLzlh_31VWEFqeTtpvodYxhOEnUFr0Nzq-

QR Code

CHAPTER 2
Link: https://www.youtube.com/playlist?list=PLzlh_31VWEFqjZ8cTSljUPFe3jg_cuuQL

QR Code

CHAPTER 3
Link: https://www.youtube.com/playlist?list=PLzlh_31VWEFqKDjSxp4-STfqxQf95Np5D

QR Code

CHAPTER 4
Link: https://www.youtube.com/playlist?list=PLzlh_31VWEFp1avLnfoicm5UN230oUD_y

QR Code

CHAPTER 5
Link: https://www.youtube.com/playlist?list=PLzlh_31VWEFpYufGWpiwqc2ZQAS0fsoHu

QR Code

CHAPTER 6
Link: https://www.youtube.com/playlist?list=PLzlh_31VWEFq63LVtoV5HlRcMPQHof7JA

QR Code

CHAPTER 7
Link: https://www.youtube.com/playlist?list=PLzlh_31VWEFoqka19unBzSGpp5MN4yhg5

QR Code

CHAPTER 8
Link: https://www.youtube.com/playlist?list=PLzlh_31VWEFp4vzJYBDtKajul4rWTvBur

QR Code

CHAPTER 9
Link: https://www.youtube.com/playlist?list=PLzlh_31VWEFrHxX2YTfTF6TYNTnr-CxJm

QR Code

CHAPTER 10
Link: https://www.youtube.com/playlist?list=PLzlh_31VWEFrJ-VsasUrJ2Ts0HAwUnmfX

QR Code